The Audacity To Try:
Dare To Dream Again

By Rashard Renfro

Published By: TamikaINK

Library of Congress Cataloging-in-Publication Data has been applied for
ISBN: 9798303906570
PRINTED IN THE UNITED STATES OF AMERICA

TABLE OF CONTENTS

FOREWORD

Dear **Audacious Dreamer,**

Receive my warm greetings of peace, hope, and joy. I am delighted and honored to have been asked by the author, Rashard Renfro, to write a foreword for his debut book, The Audacity To Try: *Dare To Dream Again.*

Because of a divine appointment with destiny, I was positioned to teach and work with him in a university setting. This was six months after he returned from a 17-year prison sentence, which began for him at 23 years of age.

He returned on purpose, with a purpose, and with a dream. I found him to be intentional, focused, resilient, and a man already on his mission to empower others to revive, resurrect, and achieve their dreams. This is the "why" for the writing of his book. Read on.

I was an eyewitness to his superior intelligence, to his discipline, to his steadfastness, to his wisdom, and uncommon favor in his life. Although humble, he walked in greatness, and we know that great people are humble and powerful.

About his talents and God-given gifts, I discovered that he was, and still is, an artist, a brilliant digital creator, a graphic designer, an innovator, an inspirational writer, and a poetic and motivational speaker who is already impacting society. He's showing up as unstoppable and amazing.

Right here, it is important to note that while working with Rashard, he never showed up as a hostile, bitter, aimless, or angry man, but he demonstrated the opposite attitudes and behaviors.

I am honored to be the first-line editor of this great work. I found it motivational, inspirational, as well as transformational. I also found it to be therapeutic because of its teachings on self-forgiveness, self-esteem, self-worth, and matters of the heart. This work skillfully reminds us of the hero that lives inside each of us and that we were born to win, especially when it comes to our dreams.

Again, the purpose of this work is to encourage others to revive, resurrect, achieve, and "Go At" their goals and dreams. Rashard wants us to pump life back into our dreams like a paramedic. And I can hear him saying, "pump-it in, pump-it in, pump-it in!"

I now challenge you, audacious dreamer, to thoroughly engage with the thoughtfully designed diagnostic questionnaires that he has presented. They will help you discover, or uncover some of your subconscious beliefs, including those that may be limiting your ability to achieve on a much higher level. Also, allow your beliefs and concepts to be supported, reconsidered, and inspired. Be motivated to receive the truths presented so that you can bring life back to your vision, goals, and dreams. By doing so, Rashard will have accomplished phase one of his mission to empower you to dare to dream again.

Now, let's applaud him for his commitment and faithfulness in getting this work out to you and the rest of the world.

Sending Blessings & Shalom,
Evangelist Lady Normell Guyden MEd, Master of Divinity
President Founder of Still Small Voice Ministries, MCT INC.
Board Certified By the American Assoc. of Christian Counselors
Published Author

"A wasteland is a barren, uncultivated, or empty area of land that is not used for building or growing crops. Wastelands can be caused by toxicity in the soil or harsh conditions."

I grew up in an area known to the locals as "The Wasteland" in a neighborhood called Glenville/St. Clair. It was a typical hood, ghetto, underserved, underprivileged, low-income community. Our community was full of gangs, drugs, murders, rapes, kidnappings, and other dangerous elements of destruction.

So how, then, does one go from growing up in the Wastelands of Cleveland, Ohio, to becoming an internationally known and well-sought-after World Champion of Public Speaking?

The duality of simplicity and involution makes my story very similar to the author's.

Both of our journeys, from adversity to empowerment, have one common theme. Resilience.

Although we were originally rooted in a wasteland, we made the choice to plant new seeds on fertile ground. We grew new roots deep into fresh soil with the necessary nutrients to properly feed our dreams.

If you want to reach higher and create a new life for yourself, this book is a necessary tool.

I have an assignment for you before starting this book. Write down, remember, and recite these three fundamentals of success daily.

1. **Everything starts within the mind**. Once I learn how to control my mind, I will learn how to control my life. When I change the way I look at things, the things I look at will change. I will be careful of what I put into my mind.

2. **I am the only one who can convince myself of my greatness.** I must positively affirm myself daily. I must build a solid relationship with myself. I will learn to love, accept, and forgive myself. My success starts with getting to know who I am and then working towards becoming the man or woman I truly want to be. No one is coming to save me. It starts with me.

3. **"If I want to go fast, go alone. If I want to go far, go together."** There are 4 E's that contribute to success: exposure, environment, education, and experience. Having a mentor, coach, or leadership figure in my life will open doors for me that I never knew existed. I will listen to sound advice, accept wise challenges, and step outside of my comfort zone. I will learn to trust the ones who are trustworthy and give distance and grace to those who have done me wrong.

Writing, remembering, and reciting these three fundamentals of success daily will help you with reprogramming your mind. I guarantee you that after

21 days of writing and reciting these words, you will start to feel an internal positive shift.

Are you ready to begin your journey from adversity to empowerment? Are you ready to transform into the man or woman you were truly created to be?

I dare you to dream again.

Ramona J. Smith
Ladybug Speaker LLC, Owner
2018 World Champion of Public Speaking

I'm sure someone in our family can pull out a picture to show that I have known Rashard Renfro since he was born. I am not old enough to remember him as an infant, but he is my little cousin. The quiet one that was quick to laugh. The smart one that often outsmarted my babysitting tactics. Our families were close when we were young. Like cousins do, we played, fought, ignored each other, bugged each other, and just *were* together. After I graduated from high school and went away to college, though, our worlds diverged. I was working on my doctorate when he went to prison. I was climbing some company's ladder as he was applying for and repeatedly denied parole. I was on a career break in Mexico when he was released, and the person that I knew started to share his mature dreams and talents with me and the rest of the world.

I am honored to write a foreword for his first book. In a world that keeps telling us to work hard for other people's dreams, Rashard has cleverly crafted these pages to remind us of the depths of strength and potential that each of us has within us. This book almost reads like a mantra for us all to use to hold ourselves up. To remember *how* to have self-esteem in the presence of doubt (and doubters) and know that *you* are the person that can be counted on to make your future a reality. It also reminds us that yes, sometimes things happen – you make a mistake, your efforts don't work out the first or the fiftieth time, someone you thought was on your side wasn't, etc. – but those things do not render our dreams null and void. On the contrary, they help us become people who are resilient enough to do the hard work of fulfilling our dreams.

Rashard's journey might seem foreign to you on the surface, but if we're honest with ourselves, it's only a different path on the diverse landscape of what it means to live as a human. Rashard's journey has brought us a person who can share how to climb out of a crucible, be realistically optimistic, and make decisions from an abundant mindset. He teaches us how to achieve dreams in real life while being honest and learning how to be better at loving yourself.

This book is so timely and relevant to our changing world. I frequently tell my mentees, staff members, and colleagues that "you are responsible for the future." That's usually followed by some admonition to stop waiting and to start doing. I love this book for providing more concrete ways to help people (including myself) to get over that hump. To dust off and breathe life into our dreams. After all, if we don't give our dreams life, we're just waiting on someone else's dream to come along and push us forward into a future we have no desire to live in.

Danielle Smith, PhD
Technology Executive
Inclusive Technology Evangelist
Public Speaker

PREFACE

"If you find yourself in a fair fight, you didn't plan your mission properly."
David Hackworth

o strive for the impossible, to grasp at the intangible, you need more than just a spark of bravery—you need a wildfire of defiance. You need the kind of audacity that laughs in the face of failure and sneers at the skeptics. They'll tell you it's a fool's goal, that you're not being realistic, that you are chasing after what can't be caught. But what do they know of the fire that burns within you? What do they understand of the steel that forges your resolve? Let them whisper their pathetic doubts. Let them cower behind their feeble "can'ts" and "shouldn'ts" while you forge your destiny with unyielding determination. Because when your ambitions have beaten you down, crushed your spirit, and left you for dead, it's not enough to get back up—you must rise with a brazen grin and defiance in your eyes.

This is the essence of a true warrior: staring down the odds, mocking the naysayers, and standing tall amidst the chaos. So, embrace the fury within, let it fuel your relentless pursuit of greatness, and leave the weak-willed trembling in your wake. For it's in the crucible of adversity, when the world seems hell-bent on breaking you, that legends are born. And with every setback, every defeat, you'll rise again, stronger and more defiant, proving to them all that you are truly unstoppable.

It's about having the raw audacity to stare fate dead in the eyes and growl, "Is that the best you've got?" It's about having the unbreakable spirit to rise from the rubble of your failures, time and time again, each time more savage, more relentless, more unstoppable—like a phoenix reborn in the flames of its destruction.

Every blow, every setback, every moment of doubt is nothing more than a test of your unwavering resolve. Remember, champions don't fold under pressure; they adapt, evolve, and overcome. Embrace the unrelenting pursuit of victory and let your hunger for success fuel your rise to greatness. So, steel yourself for the battles ahead, for it is in the heat of the fight that legends are forged. Harness your inner strength, unleash your true potential, and prove that no obstacle can stand in the way of your undeniable destiny. Never falter, never surrender, and always remember: you were born to win.

Never fold up when the fight is hard on you, no matter what you face—whether it's something small or monumental. Knuckle up and fight as hard as you can. After a while, you'll realize you're still standing, and maybe you're winning. When the world throws its best punches—when bills pile up like unpaid debts, when love turns to betrayal, when the odds stack higher than a skyscraper—don't crumple. Stand tall, even if your knees wobble. Remember, the toughest fights happen when you're already bruised, battered, and gasping for air. That's when your true mettle shines. Small or big, face it head-on. Life doesn't discriminate. It'll throw a pebble or a boulder your way and won't apologize. Maybe it's a nagging boss, a broken heart, or a mountain of unpaid bills. But guess what? The universe doesn't care. So square your shoulders, grit your teeth, and stare down your demons. Size doesn't matter; your fight does.

Imagine your knuckles—scarred, calloused, and unyielding. They're not just for throwing punches but for gripping life's slippery edges. When despair whispers, "Stay down," clench those fists. Channel your inner fighter. Swing back, even if your arms ache. Bruises heal; regret lasts forever. Fight like your life depends on it because it does. Every heartbeat, every breath—it's your battle cry. When the world blurs into chaos, focus. Block the distractions, ignore the naysayers, and unleash hell. Your sweat, your tears— they're the ink on your legacy. So fight, not because victory is guaranteed, but because surrender isn't an option. And after a while, revelation; I did it. You'll stagger, stumble, and curse the universe. But keep going. One day, you'll catch your reflection—a survivor, a warrior. You'll taste the metallic tang of resilience on your tongue. Maybe you won't be holding a trophy; perhaps it'll be a crumpled love letter or a paycheck. Condemn it, you'll know: You're still here.

Maybe you're even winning the battle now and don't know it. Victory isn't always a parade; sometimes, it's a quiet nod to survival. Look around. The scars, the stories—they're your badges of honor. Life's scoreboard isn't about knockouts; it's about endurance. So raise that weary chin, smirk at the cosmos, and say, "Yeah, I'm still standing. And victory is coming."

INTRODUCTION

"If you want to conquer fear, don't sit home and think about it."
Dale Carnegie

As of today, our names do not belong to the ages, but we do have a rendezvous with Destiny. It's a set reservation with the future image that we have of ourselves at our best, doing our best, and living the best life possible. It's the history that you shall make. The record of high achievements that the authors shall write of the future depends on your course of action to make a change today. Now, that's a change in your thinking, a change in your discipline, and a change in how you value yourself.

Now, you have an image of yourself for the future that has sent you an invitation to come to the life of greatness that awaits you. The price of that voyage, the share of the future that belongs to you, can only be paid with your immediate investment and change.

Now consider this, as one of my mentors, Corey Harris, asked me. If I were to take a new crisp hundred dollar bill and crumble it up, stomp on it a few times, and cause a few tears to it, does that hundred-dollar bill lose any value with all the hardships, tears, and changes that it has been through? It still holds value and is worth equal to a new crisp hundred dollar bill. Now, let's look at ourselves. Many of us have been stepped on and crumbled up, and some of us still have the scar tissues from the tears that we've been through. Yet, we still hold value and worth just as equal to any other historical figure. You just have to see it within yourselves. Change your perspective, and you can change your life.

Now, I have learned that greatness doesn't ask for much, just all that you've got, and as Billy Alsbrooks once said, "You can either sit around and admire the goats from the sidelines, or you can get up and become one!" To be a goat means to "Go At." So, we need to "Go At" our dreams. We need to "Go At" our plans, and we need to "Go At" our goals by head-ramming our thoughts into actions because the life of the goat, the life of a champion, and that of a true warrior is a life of competition going against elite opponents in toughest arenas. Because you have never seen or heard of a goat that is scared to bump heads, you have to be willing to dive head-first into your dreams and your goals.

Let's look at the meaning of G.O.A.T. First, the "G.O." means the "greatest of." When you apply this new concept to be the "greatest of" whatever you're doing at the moment, and when you think that this has to be the "greatest of" all performances that you've ever done and that this is the greatest of all ideas that you've ever had, you'll realize that every day is the greatest of all days that you've ever lived.

Next, the "A.T." in the word G.O.A.T means "all times." You're thinking, I must always be building on myself. I must be improving at all times and constantly breaking out of my comfort zone, going against opposition, and facing challenges at all times. Because of competition, you can't dodge any challenger. You must act like a cobra because this is how you earn heart. It's by racing champions.

You have to square up, dig your heels in, and fight back with all that you have. Keep those guards high, chin tucked, and eyes sharp because when life swings, it's aiming to lay you flat. But you? You're made of sterner stuff. You're cut from that cloth that doesn't tear easily. So, when the going gets rough, remember who you are. You're a fighter, born from the grit and grime, and you've got more heart than life's got punches. Stand tall, throw those counters, and let life know you ain't going down without a scrap. That's the only way to make it in this game. Keep swinging, keep surviving, and above all, keep your spirit unbroken.

Chapter 1
The Fight Is Not Over It's Just Begun

"If you chase anything in life, chase the things that get you excited about living.
Chase the things that give you hope, happiness and a glimpse of a better life.
Chase the things that make you want to be a better person. Chase the things that inspire you to think, create..."
Author - Unknown

Today, I want you to pick up your passion and go back to pursuing your dreams. Now, to begin with, I would like to explain how, when I was denied parole three times, I said, "Forget it." I trashed all of my plans, all of my ideas, all of my designs and writings. I also trashed this big pile of paperwork of connections, agencies, and contacts that provided aid. There were all of my dreams and ambitions, and I threw them all in the trash. I said, "Forget it all."

Now, I don't know if you ever thought like that before, but have you ever set your goals and expectations so high and received the biggest rejections? At that moment, disappointment can be a low blow or a gut shot. It may even floor you. I know that this may not apply to everyone. Some people have never had to lay their dreams to rest, but as T.D. Jakes once said in a message, "To those who once had to take inventory of your life and put your dreams way deep in the back of your mind, I want to relate to you. Hiding from yourself by burying your dreams into the deep recesses of your mind and trying to explain them away will keep you broken, fearful, and, at some levels, disappointed in yourself. To those who chased after your dream for so long that you finally gave in and said that it would never happen, and you had to declare to yourself that your dreams are dead so that you can have a moment of peace."

See, I had to fight with putting my hopes and dreams into a trashcan as a sign of regaining some form of control in dealing with my agony of defeat. But then I had to snap back to reality. I had a choice in how I would respond to that defeat. Do I give up on my prayers? Do I put my dreams in the trash and think that my God-given talents will not take me to where God wants me to be? Then I had a revelation that at this stage in life, the dreams that I held onto had been invested in far too long to be laid to rest now.

Now, notice this. Disappointment and rejection trigger a pain response in the brain. We will remember a certain pain, a loss, or a disappointment that we don't want to experience again. These things can cause us to not go after those plans or even similar goals again. So, remembering the pain stabs your dream. Remembering the losses shoots the dream down, and remembering all of the traumatic disappointments leaves the dream dead. But it's all phantom pain, and it's not real because we also have victories in pursuing our dreams. We all have experienced at least a little taste of our dreams in action before. So, we must remember all of our successes and achievements to pump back into our dreams now. We must also remember when we first found the inspiration and had the ambitious idea to go after our dream in the first place, and like a paramedic, pump it in now.

Remember the times when you were performing and executing successful actions to chase your dreams? Remember the obstacles, the practices, the studying, the watching of the pros or the experts of your dream, and pump it in.

Recall the spark that once ignited your soul and the fervent desire that set your spirit ablaze. Remember the times when success flowed through your veins as you pursued the dreams that danced before your eyes? Remember the exhilaration, the moment when the world stood still, and the heavens parted just for you? Let these memories be the defibrillator to your ambitions. Pump them in! Remember when you never felt more alive, like the skies had opened up for you, and as if the earth stopped spinning while you were losing yourself in the moment of performing your dream? Pump it in! Pump in the cheers, pump in the applause, pump in the moments when you stood victorious, and let them course through your being. Think of all the glorious moments, the triumphant victories, the uplifting times when family, friends, and even fans were cheering you, and pump it in! Pump it in! Pump it in! Pump it in! Until life is brought back into the dream.

Suddenly, the earth began to tremble. A gnarled hand, covered in dirt and decay, burst forth from the grave marked 'R.I.P. to your dreams.' The hand claws at the air, desperate for freedom, for life. This is the moment the hand bursts out from the dirt in front of the tombstone that reads R.I.P. to your dreams. This is where the buried alive emerges from the grave, throwing the dirt off its clothes and then kicking over the tombstone.

Our dreams are dead no more. Now, our dreams are more alive than ever because our dreams are back with a vengeance. They've been through hell and back. They've been shot, stabbed, left for dead, and still able to return to life. So I dare you to dream again because if Freddy Krueger is a dream killer, tell him to bring it on. We will be Michael Myers, Jason, Candyman, Sasquatch, or la Chupacabra, the real monsters are our dreams coming back to life. Remember this: our dreams are never truly dead. They are merely waiting, biding their time, ready to rise from the grave with a vengeance. And when they do, they will be more terrifying, more powerful, and more alive than ever before.

So right now, you're at a point where your dream is resurrected. It's back from the dead, and at this moment, you have this monster in your mind and in your hands. This is the time to unleash that monster and kill the game.

To illustrate this point, I'll start with a story that I read about Steve Jobs after his death. See, this is how interviews work. If you give an interview this month, it won't get published until five to six months later. So, at the time, Steve Jobs had been dead for some months, and this magazine published one of his final interviews. The picture for the article was of Steve Jobs walking through a graveyard at night with misty smoke lurking throughout. You could still see the numerous tombstones around him, but the tombstones weren't of people's names but of all the popular mobile devices until Steve Jobs came alone and killed the game. So, R.I.P. to all the MP3 players that were out until the iPod came along and killed the game. R.I.P. to all the first sleek cell phones, the flip phone, the razor phone, the blackberry, and the N-gauge that were popular until the iPhone came along and killed the game.

At that time, Apple computers were down. It was a dying company, with IBM and Dell being the top innovators, and Apple was considered primitive. Steve Jobs was even fired from the company that he co-created. His dream of Apple computers being the innovator was dead. But then Steve Jobs came to his senses. He refused to let his dream die. He went back to Apple computers with a vengeance, with the urgency to bring his dream back to life with new products to kill the game. These were the Mac, the iPod, iTunes, iPhone, Siri, and Pixar pictures, all of which killed the game.

A lot of times, you hear people say, "I'm going to kill the game." They'll say, "I'm going to kill the music game." "I'm going to kill the fashion game," "kill the restaurant game," "kill the club promoting game," and "kill the event planning game." However, the innovators called it a game changer because it caused the whole industry of that field to change up to fit their mold and follow their lead. The cell phone and smartphone designs had to change up when the iPhone came along. When the Mac Pro was released, the whole desktop computer industry had to change up to stay alive and up to par with the one that was dead just a week ago. Notice that Steve Jobs went from dream dead to dream resurrected, to killing the game. That's the blueprint!

Another example is Tyler Perry, who produced his first stage play at 21 years old in 1990 when only 30 people came to see it. Then, for six years straight, every play that he put out failed. He gave up his dream for two years. Then in 1998, he resurrected his dream to create a new stage play that sold out a 4500-seat stadium. This unleashed a monster in him to come out and kill the game, to having stage plays sell out, live shows sell out, to home videos and movies, to sitcoms, to the first movie studio owned by a black man. He went from dream dead to resurrected, to killing the game! That's the game plan! Think about it. Damien John, T.D. Jakes, Oprah Winfrey, Abraham Lincoln, and Elon Musk didn't come to play. They came to kill the game. Their direct focus, their stubborn determination, their goals that came from their biggest loss, and their biggest failure (the death of their dreams) demanded nothing less than to come back hard. They were forced to believe in themselves when no one else would. So if you're at a moment where your dreams are dead and they're just starting to come back to life for you, then you are on the right path. Things are going exactly as the course of action has been laid out for you to be able to come out and kill the game.

Chapter 2
Unleashing Your Inner Champion: A Call to Unrelenting Resilience

"Let me tell you something you already know. The world ain't all sunshine and rainbows. It's a very mean and nasty place, and I don't care how tough you are; it will beat you to your knees and keep you there permanently if you let it. You, me, or nobody is gonna hit as hard as life. But it ain't about how hard ya hit. It's about how hard you can get hit and keep moving forward. How much can you take and keep moving forward? That's how winning is done! Now, if you know what you're worth, then go out and get what you're worth. But ya gotta be willing to take the hits, and not pointing fingers saying you ain't where you wanna be because of him, or her, or anybody! Cowards do that, and that ain't you! You're better than that!"
Rocky Balboa

"Many times life will hit you hard, knock you down, and hurt you. Persevere, Never Give Up, and do your best to get up and Keep Going."
John Cena

"I've always believed that you should never, ever give up and you should always keep fighting even when there's only a slightest chance."
Michael Schumacher

Have you ever seen a movie where the star is in the big fight, the showdown battle, and he's knocked down with his opponent standing over him? The bad guy is barking at him, and he's bucking at him, and he appears out of it, unconscious to the world around him. Then the hero's corner and comrades, along with his family, yell, "Get up!" and "Get back into the fight" because it's not over yet. They're yelling his name. They're yelling Rocky, Craig from Friday, Adonis Creed, "Come on. Get up. Get back into the fight." Then, the hero stumbles up to his feet. He's bruised and bleeding, but he jumps back into the fight, giving all that he has to put his opponent on the defense. He's non-stop swinging, weaving, slipping, dipping, and countering until his opponent is on his back. Then, his family rises to their feet and cheers for his victory.

Now, let's look at ourselves; you can be knocked down and have an enemy towering over you, and the enemy may seem bigger than the room. Maybe you're fighting against a giant law firm, a competitor with more money and connections than you, or you're battling a medical condition that may seem unwinnable. They're fighting to get custody of your kids. Bills are piling up at your table. They are protesting to stop your business from opening. Then you'll hear your family, your mentors, and they all call out to you, saying, "Get up and go after your dreams. Put up a fight!" When your blood calls out to you, "Get up!" It's like an electric shock straight to the soul; you're not just going to rise; you're going to soar back into the fray like a force of nature. You're going to fight with every fiber of your being, not just throwing punches but rewriting the rules of the fight. It will cause you to muster up the strength to get up and go after your opponent with all that you've got and give them the fight of your life. I don't care if your legs don't work as well as they used to, or you have arthritis where you can't make a fist, but you can still bite them, or head butt them. You can still put up a fight. You may not have a top-notch lawyer, but you go in with your self-written legal motions. You don't have the full staff yet, but you open your business anyway, filling in where needed: manager, janitor, cash register clerk, and owner. You can still put up a fight because it's not over with.

You've been dealt a bad hand, and now you're down. You're there, on the ground, feeling like the world's got the upper hand, with the concrete cold beneath you, and the heavy breath of adversity is hot on your neck. The villains of your story are standing tall, thinking they've claimed victory. But they don't know you. They don't know that inside you is a fighter born from the struggle, shaped by the hard knocks. You pushed yourself up, every bruise a lesson, every scar a story. Now you're back in the fight, swinging with the ferocity that only comes from being down and out.

You're relentless, a force to be reckoned with, until those towering over you are looking up from the canvas. They don't know about the strength you've hidden away, the kind forged in the fires of life's toughest moments.

It's time to face the real world's reality! When life gets tough, we don't get to fold like the pampered privileged others. No matter what problems you're up against, whether a minor inconvenience or a seemingly insurmountable obstacle, you grit your teeth and fight with everything you've got. We are cut differently. You plant your feet, clench your fists, and embrace the fury that burns within. You unleash that raw, unbridled power on whatever stands in your way. And when the dust settles, and the chaos clears, you'll find yourself still standing, bloodied but unbowed, a testament to your unyielding tenacity.

Every blow, setback, and moment of doubt is just another chance to prove your strength and show the world that you're not some pathetic pushover. You're a fighter and fighters don't quit when the going gets tough. They adapt, they overcome, and they rise above the fray. So go against all the odds, forget the naysayers, and drown out the voice in your head that tells you to give up. Tap into your primal, untamed potential, and let the world know that nothing—and no one—can stand in the way of your undeniable destiny. Embrace the relentless pursuit of victory, and never forget that you were born to conquer.

When life's got you on the ropes, you don't just curl up and cry for mercy. No matter the size or scale of the beast you're facing, you summon your inner warrior and fight like there's no tomorrow. You've got an indomitable spirit within you, and it's high time you let that beast loose. Unleash your fury on whatever dares to stand in your way and watch as the chaos crumbles before your might. Every blow, setback, and moment of doubt are nothing but fodder for your unbreakable resolve.

For every defeat is a crucible, and every setback is a battle scar that only serves to harden your resolve. Let them doubt; let them cower in the shadows of their own fear, for your indomitable will shall be immortalized in the annals of legend. So stand tall, warriors, and let your defiance echo through the ages. Embrace the savage audacity to rise repeatedly, each time more ferocious, determined, and invincible, as you etch your name into the stone of history. In this concrete jungle, where the weak are devoured, and only the strong survive, audacity isn't just a trait—it's your armor, weapon, and war cry. It's the very essence of your being, the core of your soul, that refuses to be extinguished.

So wear your audacity like a badge of honor. Brandish it like a sword against the naysayers. Because in the end, it's the audacious who make history, who change the world, who become legends in a city that never forgets. Embrace the audacity, for it is the lifeblood of the extraordinary, the fuel of the fearless, the legacy of the legends. Dare to do the impossible, for it is in the heart of audacity that greatness is born.

I want you to close your eyes for a moment and picture the grand finale of the greatest movie you've ever seen. Imagine the quick draw duel at sundown in the dusty streets of the Wild West. Imagine the epic face-off with the Grand Master in the ancient dojos of martial arts movies. Imagine the courageous slaying of dragons in the mystical realms of fantasy and, my favorite, the heart-pounding explosions of buildings with the supervillains of action movies.

Now, open your eyes because this isn't just a scene from a movie. This is your life. You are the hero of your epic tale. And just like in those movies, the resolution, the reason, and the purpose of the battle's outcome come after the big fight. The villain has been a tyrannical leader. He's been an obstacle blocking an entrance or passage.

Now, the hero gets the chance to move in to rescue his girl, save his kid, and restore peace to the community. But it's still one last minor fight for the hero because the credits haven't begun to roll just yet. He still has to snip the wires to destroy the bomb tied to his child. It's the moment where you must snip the wires of doubt to free your potential. It's where he has to pull up his wife, who's screaming at the top of her lungs because she's hanging from her fingertips on the edge of a building. It's where you have to pull up your ambition that's hanging by a thread, screaming for realization. But remember, it's not over just yet. The credits haven't begun to roll. You still have one last fight, one final hurdle to overcome.

We are all on a hero's journey, and the hero must win in the end. So we must win if we are the hero of our story. Our journey will be filled with showdowns, face-offs, boss fights, and cliffhangers. But these moments define us, pushing us to climb to the top, to the climax of our struggle, to the pinnacle of our goals. You may feel that you're past the hardest part, "The Big Fight," and you're so close to the reward that it's within reach. You've got all the degrees, certifications, and accolades. Now, it's time to step out into the field and succeed.

You won the bid to have the building for your business; now, you must draw in the customers to make your business thrive. You wrote a book or song and had it published or copyrighted. Now, you must promote it to make it a bestseller. Your resolution is within arm's reach while your heart is still pounding from the big fight. What brought you this far, and what won the showdown, is not what is needed to get you to the reward. You must gain the momentum of the hero's journey, using each victory to propel you forward, building up speed as the rotten planks of doubt fall away with every step you take, racing across to the other side to success.

Ladies and gentlemen, I want you to stand up right now. Stand up and feel the ground beneath your feet, because that ground is where legends are born. It's where you stand, not as a person who's been knocked down but as a warrior who's risen again and again. This is what we do—we bounce back. You can't hold us down. We keep pushing through. These aren't just words; these are the undeniable facts of your life. Think about it. How many of you have clawed your way out of poverty, risen from the ashes of bankruptcy, or emerged stronger from the pain of a bitter divorce?

You're still here, standing, rising, constantly coming from the bottom. You're not just getting by; you're getting it from your resources, coming out of one battle and heading straight into another. This fighting spirit, this resilience, is what defines us. We go against all odds. We walk through fire and come out not just unscathed but wet-drenched in the victory of our perseverance. This is the essence of who we are.

We must keep this victory momentum going. It's a personal power pace, a rhythm that beats within every one of us. With every battle, you gain more energy and more confidence because what you're doing is compounding courage. You're compounding trust in your abilities. Remember, every setback is a setup for a comeback. Every defeat is just a prelude to your next triumph. And every challenge is an opportunity to prove to the world, but most importantly, to prove to yourself that you have what it takes. So keep fighting, keep striving, and keep trusting in your boundless potential because you are a champion, and champions never stay down.

I would like for you to imagine this movie scene: You're standing at the edge of a skyscraper, the embodiment of your conquered fears and defeated limitations. The villain, the symbol of every challenge you've faced, lies vanquished at your feet. You've just conquered your greatest adversary, and now it's time to make your escape from the treacherous grounds you've battled upon. You find yourself on the precipice of a towering skyscraper; below, the city sprawls out like a canvas of possibilities, each light a beacon of potential. The helicopter above is your next step; the ladder hanging from it is a bridge to your future. It's just out of reach, but you've come too far to let this moment slip through your fingers. With the resolve of the ages, you surge forward, leaping into the air with a faith that defies gravity. With your fingers, mere inches from the rung, and with the full force of your will, you leap. It's a moment of pure terror, a test of faith where everything you've worked for hangs in the balance. With every ounce of determination and focus you possess, you leap towards salvation. Your fingers stretch out to the ladder, swaying like a serpent from the helicopter. For a heartbeat, you touch salvation. It's cold metal against your skin. You feel the victory, the sweet touch of success. As you close your hand to form a fist grip around the rung of the ladder your grasp slips and now you are falling. As you plummet, the wind is roaring in your ears. And through tunnel vision, the ground appears to be rushing up to collide with your face with tremendous force. Then suddenly a hand reaches out from the chaos, looming forward from a window. A lifeline amidst the descent. When all seems lost, it's not the impersonal hand of fate; it's the warm, firm grip of someone who's been with you every step of the way. It's family and friends, the ones who've believed in you even when you've doubted yourself. They're not just observers; they're participants in your journey, ready to catch you, to pull you back from the brink, because this journey—your journey—is not a solitary one. This is the moment of truth, where faith meets fate, where the hero's journey is crystallized not in the solitary act of triumph, but in the unity of struggle and salvation. It's a vivid reminder that our battles are shared, our falls are caught, and our victories are collective. This is the power of connection, the strength of unity. Your journey has never been just about you. It's about the bonds you've formed, and the support you've given and received. It's about the shared victories and the collective resilience. So as you cling to that hand, know that you're not just holding on to safety. You're holding on to the truth that we are stronger together, that our dreams are not solitary pursuits, but collective endeavors. This is your moment to recognize that every leap of faith is made possible by the hands ready to catch us. Now, rise with the support that surrounds you, and step into the destiny that awaits. Together, you are unstoppable.

Our battles are not fought alone. Our victories are not celebrated in isolation. We fight for ourselves, yes, but we also fight for our loved ones. For our partners, for our parents, for our children, for our teams. It's about sharing the laughter with those who have shared tears, breaking bread with those who have known hunger, and celebrating together because the fight is never over just for you. For your partner, the fight continues. For your children, the battle rages on until the very end. And that's the beauty of our journey. It's a tapestry woven from the threads of shared experiences, mutual struggles, and collective triumphs. So remember, as you face your challenges, as you strive for greatness, you are never alone. The strength of those who stand with you, the power of the bonds that unite you, these are the forces that will propel you forward. These are the ties that will lift you up when you fall.

And when you rise, you rise together. Stronger, braver, and with an unbreakable spirit. Because in this life, the true victory is not just in overcoming the obstacles but in doing so hand in hand with those who matter most. Together, you are invincible. Together, you will soar.

So stand tall, and embrace the hero within you. Let each triumph be the wind at your back, pushing you towards the horizon of your dreams. The journey may be fraught with peril, but the glory at the end is worth every challenge. Keep fighting, keep striving, and above all, keep believing, because you are the hero of your story, and your story is one of victory. Now go out there and seize your destiny!

Chapter 3
I Hope That You Fail

"Every adversity, every failure, every heartache carries with it the seed of an equal or greater benefit."
Napoleon Hill

I want you to listen to me, really listen. I'm going to say something that might shock you: I hope you fail. Yes, you heard me right. I hope that as you chase your dreams and as you use your God-given talents, you meet failure head-on. Because it's in failure that the seeds of success are grown. Think about Thomas Edison, who faced 6,000 failures before that lightbulb flickered to life. Consider the Wright brothers, who crashed hundreds of times before they soared. Reflect on Elon Musk, who's faced setback after setback in his quest to revolutionize our world. These aren't just stories; they're roadmaps to greatness.

You might think I'm crazy or even cruel for wishing failure upon you. But let me tell you, psychology has shown that failure is one of the greatest motivators. That near miss, that almost victory, is not the end; it's the beginning. It's the fuel that ignites the fire within you, the voice that says, "I didn't really lose. I'm just getting started." How many times have you seen a team lose by a single field goal and thought, "We didn't lose; we were just one kick away"? How often have you played a game and said, "I didn't really lose; you only won by five points"? Even the guy who gets knocked out in a fight might stand up and say, "I was winning until that guy hit me with that lucky punch."

That's the spirit I'm talking about. Coming close to your goal doesn't diminish you; it amplifies your desire to win. It makes the rematch, the next attempt, even more thrilling. You find yourself saying, "Let's run that back. Watch me win this next one." And in that moment, you're more alive than ever, rushing back into the fray, eager for victory.

Failure isn't a setback; it's a setup. It's a setup for a comeback. It empowers you and gives you confidence because now you know you can do better. That almost success isn't a loss. It's an invitation to take extreme, intense action. It's where having a near miss of your goal or an almost victory may feel partially painful, but mostly, it can make you feel motivated. So, just coming so close to your goal can make you view your chances of winning much higher for the rematch, and for the next shot at your goals. Have you ever caught yourself saying *let's run that game back? Watch me win this next one.*

At that moment, you can't wait to get back at it. You're in a dire rush to try again for victory. You can't wait for the next shot at your goal. That failure had empowered you. That failure has given you more confidence by just knowing or believing that you can do better in the next shot at your goal. What that *almost* success did was to encourage you to not only take action but to take extreme and intense action. So, just coming so close to success and having a failure can force you to feel good about yourself. Also, the direct determination that comes from an almost win, or the just barely fail, is more powerful than an almost failure or the *just won by the skin of your teeth* victory.

Picture this: You're in the ring with Bruce Lee, the legend himself. The match is intense; every move is a dance of destiny. And by some stroke of luck, you win. But it's a Pyrrhic victory, won by the skin of your teeth. Would you feel confident about a rematch? No, you wouldn't. Because deep down, you know it was a fluke. Now, flip the script. Imagine you are barely lost, and Bruce Lee won by a hair's breadth. That's when something incredible happens inside you. You burn for a rematch. You're ready to go full throttle, holding nothing back because now, the real competition isn't Bruce Lee—it's your past performance. It's the voice inside you saying, "You didn't beat me; I beat myself." That's right. You're out to prove that it wasn't your opponent or any obstacle that caused your defeat. It was a momentary lapse, a slip of focus, something from within, not from without.

When you aim for a lofty goal and fall short, you don't accept defeat. You say, "I have to give it another try. I will not lose this time. Failure is not an option." You'll say, "Just give me another chance at my goals. Give me another shot at my dreams, another opportunity to bring my A-game and watch me crush it!"

Let me give you an example. Imagine that you set a goal to do 1,000 push-ups or 1,000 jumping jacks. You get to 850, and then there's a call for the gym to shut down, and you think to yourself, "Not now; I'm so close to my goal." So you pump out another 50 or another 75 until it's time to go to the door, but you didn't make it to the 1,000 goal. It's a failure, but you don't see it as a failure because you now know it can be done. Your mind doesn't comprehend that you failed. You didn't process that you had a loss because you now know you have it in you to succeed. And because you now know you have what it takes, you see that failure has proven to you that *you can*, and you will succeed in another try.

It is these types of failures and mistakes that can give you the ammunition to go back into the same battlefield where you had your most recent defeat, and instantly, you no longer notice any failures in your actions to reach your goal. When we reach that level where we have the audacity to push through obstacles constantly, and to ignore failures until our goal is obtained, then we will have the champion's mindset. It's this perspective where we don't see failure but the next move to get to success.

Now, I want you to imagine this scenario: You're trapped in a burning house, and the flames are growing and spreading around you. You're starting to feel the heat begin to scorch your skin, and the smoke is starting to fill your lungs, thus making it hard for you to breathe. You know you need some air, so giving in isn't an option. Any failed attempts within the past few moments to save your very own life don't matter.

When trying to kick down the front door failed you, when trying to dash the flames with water failed you, when trying to call the fire department failed you, all of that failure doesn't matter because it's about moving on to what's the next best thing that's going to keep you alive. And in that instance, in that moment, you have the ultimate revelation that you would not die like this but that you need to succeed at getting out because your life depends on it. You can't just fan at the flames like you kind of want to live. No! You're going to have to kick out the glass window. When that doesn't work, you'll grab your TV, your Xbox, the PS5, your Mac Pro, the kitchen sink, your 45, and anything that you can to smash that window to get you out. Then you're out in the open air, coughing the smoke out of your lungs. Success at last because you wanted it bad enough and because you found what was most important over any failures or prize possessions that you have. It's because you became aware that you are going to succeed or die trying.

Now, apply this to your life. What do you want? What's your burning house? Is it that dream job? That relationship? That goal you've been chasing? Whatever it is, want it as your life depends on it. Kick down doors, break glass ceilings, and grab life by the collar because you're not here to play small. You're here to thrive. Remember, success isn't a spectator sport. It's a full-contact, all-in, no-holds-barred battle. So go out there and want it—as bad as you want to live. And that, my friends, is how you turn desperation into determination. Now go forth and conquer!

Notice that when you're under pressure to live a certain way, and when you decide that you will not die like this, you will get up and "go at" your goals. It has to get this serious. It has to get that real to you. You are supposed to have goosebumps throughout your body, your heart is supposed to sink to your stomach, and the hair is supposed to stand at the back of your neck because this is serious business here. We're talking about conquering your dreams.

Chapter 4
The Invitation To Forgive Yourself

"Forgive yourself for not knowing what you didn't know before you learned it."
Maya Angelou

In the presence of our own histories, our own mistakes, and our own triumphs, each of us carries the weight of moments we wish we could rewrite. But today, I want to talk to you about the power of self-forgiveness and the grace of healing oneself. Imagine standing in front of a mirror, not to scrutinize the flaws but to embrace them. I want you to see not just a reflection, but a person worthy of love and forgiveness—yourself. Self-forgiveness is not a sign of weakness; it is the epitome of strength. It is the beginning of healing, the first step towards a future unburdened by the chains of past regrets. Let us take a lesson from the earth itself. After the fiercest storms, the sun rises again, flowers bloom, and life begins anew. The earth does not dwell on the havoc wrought by the storm; it forgives and nurtures life once more. We must learn to do the same. To forgive ourselves is to allow the sun to rise within us, to let our inner gardens bloom.

Remember, forgiving oneself is not about forgetting the past but about building the future. It's about acknowledging that even in our darkest moments, we are still capable of light. It's about recognizing that growth is not just possible; it is inevitable—if we allow ourselves the space to heal. So, let us make a promise today to ourselves and to each other to be kinder to the person we see in the mirror. Let's understand that every scar is a lesson, and every flaw, is a story of survival. Let us vow to move forward not with heavy hearts but with lightness and hope. For in the words of the wise, 'To err is human; to forgive, divine.' And what could be more divine than forgiving the very person who needs it most? Ourselves.

In the pursuit of wholeness and inner peace, there comes a pivotal moment when you must summon the courage to forgive. But it is not merely the forgiveness of others that sets you free—it is the profound act of forgiving yourself. True liberation comes when you release the weight of regret, confront the shadows of your past, and emerge victorious. It takes immense bravery to face yourself, to engage in that ultimate battle, and to shatter the chains that have held you captive for so long. Ego and pride will be cast aside as you embrace the transformative power of self-forgiveness. You will rise, reborn, as your higher self takes flight.

As you embark on this journey towards closure, remember that it is an act of profound strength to confront your own vulnerabilities and to extend forgiveness inward. Only then can you truly find the freedom to heal, to grow, and to embrace the limitless potential that lies within you.

So, stand tall, dear friend, and take that courageous step towards self-forgiveness. Let go of the burdens that have weighed you down and embrace the newfound lightness of being. For it is in forgiving yourself that you will discover the power to create a brighter, more authentic future—one that reflects the resilient spirit that has carried you this far.

The moment you find closure and when you feel complete is when you forgive yourself. There is a certain power that only comes when you forgive yourself, but not when you forgive an abusive father, an emotionally neglected mother, a brother who stole from you, a sister who lied to you, a spouse who cheated on you, or a child who disappointed you. You only find your closure when you forgive yourself and when you give yourself the freedom of no regrets, which enables you to never feel sorry for yourself anymore.

It takes a great amount of courage to stand up to yourself and have the final battle with yourself and with what has been holding you back for years. It is the ultimate war of all wars that will annihilate your ego, eradicate your pride, and resurrect your higher self.

The power that it takes to forgive yourself will unleash a greater power so ultimate within you that you will wish that you can do it again and again. The freedom that comes from forgiving yourself will give you all the ammunition, energy, and drive to conquer your purpose. The next step to going beyond your past and into your greater future self is in forgiving yourself. There is no use in hoping for a better childhood or better experiences of your past or any past mistakes that could've been better handled. There is nothing so extreme that you have to constantly feel guilty and feel ashamed of. The time to forgive yourself is now. The time to free yourself from guilt and shame is now. The time to be released from your past is now.

As you stand at the edge of change, know that the power to forgive yourself will unleash a force within you so potent, so transformative, that you'll find yourself yearning to experience it time and time again. This liberating act of self-forgiveness will provide you with the tools, energy, and determination to conquer your purpose and step boldly into your greater future self. There is no need to cling to the hope of a different past or to dwell on experiences that could have been. The time has come to release yourself from the burdens of guilt and shame that have weighed you down for far too long. Embrace the power of self-forgiveness, for it holds the key to unlocking your true potential.

Do not let the ghosts of your past define you or dictate your path forward. Instead, gather your strength and courage to face them head-on, granting yourself the grace and compassion that you so readily extend to others. By forgiving yourself, you break the chains of regret and create space for healing, growth, and personal evolution.

The moment to free yourself from the shackles of your past is now. I cannot repeat that enough. No mistake, no misstep, is too great to overcome when you embrace the transformative power of self-forgiveness. Let your past be a testament to your resilience. And let your future be a beacon of hope, guiding you toward a life of authenticity, purpose, and lasting fulfillment. In our quest for personal growth and mental fortitude, we must confront the stark reality of who we are. To cease the detrimental cycle of self-deception, we must acknowledge the behaviors and consequences that have shaped our character. No longer can we hide behind facades or bury our vulnerabilities in the depths of our subconscious.

Self-confession is a transformative journey that illuminates our true selves, fostering an environment of honesty, empathy, and understanding. It is through this raw, unguarded exploration of our innermost thoughts and feelings that we can begin to heal the fractures within our psyche and mend the relationships around us. Create a safe space for yourself, be it a quiet moment of solitude, the pages of your journal, or a private recording. Here, confess your secrets, your emotions, and the pain that weighs heavy on your heart. Surrender to the knowledge that, in this sacred space, you are free from judgment, rejection, or betrayal.

In your confession, unveil the actions or inactions that have led to feelings of shame or guilt. Acknowledge the aspects of yourself that you have long tried to conceal. It is through this bold act of vulnerability that you can begin to forgive and accept yourself, embracing your humanity and the imperfections that make you whole.

As you embark on this courageous journey, remember that the ultimate goal is not to punish yourself for past mistakes but to foster growth, self-compassion, and understanding. By laying bare the depths of your soul, you will discover the courage to face life's challenges with authenticity, honesty, and resilience.

It is in this sacred space of self-confession and forgiveness that you will find the strength to rebuild your mentality and step forward into the light, no longer bound by the shadows of your past. Self-confession is a transformative journey that illuminates our true selves, fostering an environment of honesty, empathy, and understanding. It is through this raw, unguarded exploration of our innermost thoughts and feelings that we can begin to heal the fractures within our psyche and mend the relationships around us.

Confessing to yourself the brutal truth of who you truly are and drastically stopping lying to yourself that you are not the person that you created yourself to be in your mind, is detrimental to rebuilding a new mentality. Acknowledge your behavior and the consequences that you create for your character and personality. You will no longer be hiding behind a put-on face to display to the world. You may have come to the point where you pushed your behavior into the deep corners of your unconscious that you may have tried to explain away. Hiding from ourselves by pushing our behavior into the deep corners of our conscience or trying to explain away our vulnerabilities keeps us broken, full of fear, and, at some level, afraid of who we truly are. It makes us dishonest to ourselves and, therefore, unable to deal with others and with society outside of us.

Confessing to yourself is your journey to find your truth. It is to stop lying to yourself about your behavior and its consequences. Confessing allows you to consciously decide who you truly are. So, you have to think about yourself and think about your thinking and come to know and accept your faults and needs. You can mentally confess in solitude when you open your heart. Writing in your journal flows easily when you open your heart. You can look into the mirror or the camera on your phone and record a video making a confession to yourself.

Confess your secrets. Confess your emotions. Confess your pain and shame that you do not feel safe to share with anyone else. Just surrender to yourself. With a certain knowledge, you will not be rejected or betrayed when you're speaking to yourself since it will only be you and God who know what you are recording, saying, and writing.

Forgiveness begins with acknowledging the weight of our actions or inactions. Once we voice our confessions, we confront the reality of how we might have wronged ourselves or others. This realization may bring about a sense of guilt for deeds perceived as unforgivable or for failings and embarrassments we've kept hidden within our personal boundaries. Yet, it is precisely in this moment of self-confession that we must find the courage to release these burdens. By admitting our faults to ourselves, we take the first step towards self-forgiveness, allowing us to move forward with compassion and understanding.

Referring to the recording of our confession and seeing ourselves looking into our eyes in that vulnerable moment, can give us a clarity that we would not have gotten if we were only thinking about the issue. Accepting your truth, accepting your pain, and accepting your healing will be the awakening of a new you.

In life, we often encounter experiences that leave us feeling broken, lost, and uncertain of our ability to carry on. Few events are as deeply wrenching as a devastating breakup, which can upend the foundations of our world and cast doubt upon our self-worth. Yet, even in the depths of heartbreak lies the potential for profound transformation and personal growth. When a relationship ends, we are left with shattered dreams and an overwhelming sense of grief. The person we once loved and trusted with our hearts is no longer by our side, and the future we envisioned together has been irrevocably altered. It is natural to question our values and wonder if we will ever find love again.

However, within the pain of heartbreak lies an opportunity for self-discovery. As we sift through the rubble of our past relationship, we can begin to identify patterns and behaviors that may have contributed to its downfall. In recognizing these patterns, we can work to address them, fostering personal growth and resilience that will serve us in all aspects of our lives. As we heal, we must be kind to ourselves, offering the same compassion and support we would extend to a friend in need. This is a time for self-care and reflection, a chance to rediscover our strengths and passions. By embracing this period of introspection, we create a foundation for a brighter, more fulfilling future.

While it may seem unfathomable in the throes of heartache, there will come a day when we can look back on this experience with gratitude. For it is through the crucible of pain that we are reborn, emerging stronger and wiser than before. We may even come to see that the end of this relationship was, in fact, a blessing in disguise. It was a breakthrough that set us on a path toward our true purpose and a love that is deeper and more fulfilling than we ever imagined. So, if you find yourself navigating the tumultuous waters of heartbreak, remember that you are not alone. Take comfort in the knowledge that this experience, as difficult as it may be, holds within it the seeds of transformation. Embrace the journey of healing and self-discovery, and trust that, in time, you will emerge from this experience with newfound strength, wisdom, and a heart that is open to the boundless possibilities of love.

I want you to take a moment and think about the power of forgiveness. Not just forgiving others but forgiving yourself. We all make mistakes. We all stumble and fall. But it's not the falling that defines us; it's the getting back up. It's the lessons we learn, the strength we gain, and the resilience we build. But sometimes, we hold onto our mistakes. We let them define us. We carry them around like a heavy burden, and they weigh us down. But I'm here to tell you it's time to let go. It's time to forgive yourself. Forgiving yourself is not about forgetting the mistakes you've made; it's about learning from them. It's about recognizing that you are not your mistakes.

You are not your past. You are a person of immense worth and potential, and every day is a new opportunity to grow and change. Self-forgiveness is a journey of healing. It's a journey of self-discovery, of self-love, and self-improvement. It's about recognizing that you are human, that you are flawed, and that's okay. Because it's our flaws that make us unique. It's our flaws that make us human. So, let's embark on this journey together. Let's learn to forgive ourselves, to love ourselves, and to grow from our mistakes. Because when we do, we will find that we are not just healing ourselves, we are also healing the world around us. Remember, you have the power to forgive, to heal, and to change. And that power starts with forgiving yourself.

Chapter 5
Step Out Of Your Comfort Zone

"I used to have a comfort zone where I knew I wouldn't fail.
The same four walls and busy work were really more like jail.
I longed so much to do the things I'd never done before,
But stayed inside my comfort zone and paced the same old floor.
I said it didn't matter that I wasn't doing much.
I said I didn't care for things like commission checks and such.
I claimed to be so busy with the things inside the zone,
But deep inside I longed for something special of my own.
I couldn't let my life go by just watching others win.
I held my breath; I stepped outside and let the change begin.
I took a step and with new strength I'd never felt before,
I kissed my comfort zone goodbye and closed and locked the door.
If you're in a comfort zone, afraid to venture out,
Remember that all winners were at one time filled with doubt.
A step or two and words of praise can make your dreams come true.

Reach for your future with a smile; success is there for you!"
Author-Unknown

"Life begins at the end of your comfort zone." -
Neale Donald Walsch

I offer you an invitation to step out of your comfort zone today. To live the life that you always wanted, you're going to have to start living a different life. You have to start doing something extra out of the ordinary to live the extraordinary. You can't keep doing what is normal and comfortable to you and expect some changes and something out of the normal to happen. You can't make a change stuck in your comfort zone. You can't see growth doing your ordinary. You can't become trapped in what you know. So, to unearth and discover the talents you have inside, you have to step out of your comfort zone and try new things, journey to new locations, meet new people, and have motivational talks to get up and go get it. How else will you ever know every aspect of yourself if you don't test out your ideas, talents, and what is inside you?

Consider that a flower starts as a seed in a hard shell that it must push through to begin growth. The sprouting bud then must continue to push through dirt, climbing up against what has been foundation long before it was there. Then, the sprouting bud pushes through, being buried to emerge above ground, going against all sources of blockage.

Notice that you can become trapped in what you know, and where you'll be stuck in your familiar and stagnant in your normal. It's easy to become complacent and stagnant in the face of adversity, allowing our fears and insecurities to hold us back. However, we must remember that we are capable of so much more than we give ourselves credit for. Being stagnant is like standing still in the midst of a vast, ever-changing hurricane. When we stand still, we cannot advance or move forward. To progress and evolve, we must break through the barriers that seek to hinder our growth.

Like a delicate flower, we must find the strength within ourselves to push through the soil, reaching for the light that nurtures our development. Established foundations and blockages may try to impede our progress, but we must remain steadfast in our pursuit of growth. When God shines a light on our path, we are empowered to overcome any obstacle that comes our way. We must embrace this divine guidance and use it as fuel to drive our personal evolution. As we continue to grow and push through the barriers that once seemed insurmountable, we will uncover new facets of our strength and resilience.

Each challenge we face is an opportunity to learn and expand our understanding of ourselves and the world around us. By refusing to remain stagnant, we open ourselves up to new experiences, relationships, and perspectives that enrich our lives and contribute to our personal growth. To fully embrace the journey of life, we must be willing to step out of our comfort zones and confront our fears. Remember that you are not alone in this endeavor. Seek support from friends, family, or mentors who can offer guidance and encouragement along the way. So, as you navigate the winding roads of life, always strive to move forward and grow. Embrace the lessons that come from overcoming obstacles, and remember that, with determination and faith, you can break through any barrier that stands in your way.

In the natural world, we find a beautiful metaphor for our own journey through life. Consider the delicate flower, awakening at the break of day, unfurling its petals to embrace the sun's life-giving rays. In the presence of the sun, the flower flourishes, reaching new heights as it grows stronger and more vibrant. However, as the sun dips below the horizon and twilight descends, the flower folds its petals and lowers its head. Without the sun's guidance, the flower rests, awaiting the dawn of a new day to bloom once again.

Much like the flower, we, too, must learn to lift our heads and open our hearts to the guidance that nurtures our growth. In seeking wisdom from mentors, role models, and the divine light of a higher power, we find the strength and courage to pursue our passions and fulfill our purpose. When we are blessed with guidance, we must be mindful of the opportunities it presents and embrace the lessons it imparts. By following the examples set by those who inspire us, we discover our true potential and cultivate the qualities that make us unique and extraordinary. However, there may be times when we feel alone or uncertain, as though the light that once guided us has faded away. In these moments, remember that the wisdom you have gained from those who have shown their light upon you is not lost. Their guidance remains within you, providing solace and direction during life's darkest hours.

As we navigate the ebb and flow of life, let us be like the flower, gracefully lifting our heads to the light that illuminates our path. Let us embrace the guidance that surrounds us and find solace in knowing that, even in the absence of light, the wisdom we have gained will sustain us until dawn breaks once again. In doing so, we honor the mentors and role models who have shaped our lives, and we forge a legacy of growth, resilience, and purpose that will inspire generations to come.

You may have a "Sputnik moment" where a challenge to face failure may guide you to your purpose. When the space race to be the first to go out of space, was challenged by nations around the world, Russia was first, with their Sputnik, to go out of space, leaving America, China, Germany, and other countries in the space race as if they didn't have the right mind to figure it out. At that moment, JFK said America would be the first to go to the moon. But also, at that time, America couldn't even get into the atmosphere like Russia, yet America was challenged to go out of space and fell short.

JFK said, "We will surpass the form challenge and go further." He knew NASA had the right minds, the right equipment, and the right technology to do it all, although they didn't know how to execute it yet. Knowing that facing a few failures at the attempt until it was right, it would get done, and America became the first country to go to the moon. And that's what we call a "Sputnik Moment."

You may have a Sputnik moment when someone blurts out an idea that seems too far-fetched for them to achieve. It could also be a product or service that someone may say, "I can't wait until they develop an item or service that does this or that." You might hear someone blurt out, "I can't wait until they make doing a certain chore easier."

When you hear those types of statements, they spark your mind to think, "Hey, I can do that. I can create that product, that service, that item. I can be the one that creates that app, that book, that movie, that song, etc. I can be the one, not "they," to create it." Also, there could be problems that need to be solved when hearing sayings like -I can't wait until "they" stop doing this, or I can't wait until "they" stop making that." These statements can spark an idea for you.

Have you ever thought that a company or business should develop a new or improved product that caters to a bigger and better mass of people? And that product never comes out or happens? It could be your purpose to be the one who creates it.

Larry Page wanted a better web browser than Yahoo or Netscape, and so he created Google. Steve Jobs wanted a better yet smaller MP3 player, so he combined all the great features of all the MP3 players at that time into one product that became the iPod. So think about the service or product that should have been created by now that you don't see anywhere, like hologram video games, VR headsets, social media networks, holograms, smartphones, medication for back pain, laws for corrupt police, etc. You can be the person who builds it or combines the right group of minds to create the next big device, social-media platform, the next advanced technology, the next breakthrough medicine for disease, or even the next political movement rally.

The things that you don't like and the things that make you unhappy are also things to look at. Regarding things that you would never look at or do, the opposite of those things can lead you to know what your calling may be. Make a list of those things. Also, discuss how to combat what you hate. Many people find their purpose in fighting against what they don't like. Are you against racism, unjustified homicide, police shooting, mass incarceration, poverty, child abuse, and so forth? You can be an activist against those things or an abolitionist creating movements to stop what you hate.

Embark on a journey of self-discovery, a quest to unveil the essence of your being. This is not just an exercise; it's a revelation, a seven-day odyssey to the core of your existence. Today, we begin.

Day One: The Mirror of Friendship
Your friends are a reflection of your universe. Observe them. How do they solve problems? What visions do

they hold for their future, their children, and their community? Their discourse is a mirror reflecting back at you. If they speak of growth, savings, and community, it shows a maturity that you share. If their topics are trivial, so too might be your focus. Aim higher, seek depth, and let the reflection of your friends be one of ambition and intellect.

Day Two: The Mirror of Occupation

Your job, your career—does it ignite a fire within you? Do your colleagues recognize your innovation and your drive? Or is it just a means to an end? If your passion lies outside your work, it's time to reflect. Your true calling may be hidden in the interactions, the networks you build, and the lives you touch. Seek purpose in every task and every connection, and let your occupation reflect your true potential.

Day Three: The Mirror of Partnership

Turn to your spouse, your partner. Do they inspire you to reach new heights? Or do you find motivation within? Perhaps your partner's unwavering belief in your abilities propels you forward. Their encouragement becomes the wind beneath your wings, lifting you to places you never dreamed possible. Their compliments, heartfelt, mirror their faith in your potential.

But what about the moments when you look inward when you draw strength from your well of determination and resilience? In those times, you become your muse. Your inner fire burns bright, fueled by the desire to achieve, to overcome, to create. You find motivation within, tapping into a wellspring of purpose that transcends external validation. And so, the dance between inspiration and self-motivation continues—a delicate balance that shapes your journey.

Help them find their purpose, as they help you find yours. Imagine this reciprocity: You guide your partner toward their passions, their hidden talents, and their unexplored dreams. You become their compass, pointing them toward fulfillment. And in return, they do the same for you. Together, you navigate the labyrinth of purpose, hand in hand. Together, create a reflection of mutual support, ambition, and love. In this shared space, you weave a tapestry of love and ambition. Your dreams interlace with theirs, forming a beautiful mosaic of mutual growth. The support you offer becomes the scaffolding for their aspirations, and vice versa. So, take a moment. Reflect on your partner, your confidant, your fellow traveler. Celebrate the dance of inspiration and self-motivation. And remember that love, when nurtured with purpose, can move mountains.

Day Four: The Mirror of Self

Look in the mirror. Beyond the outfit, beyond the facade, who do you see? A person on the brink of greatness, poised to find their purpose. Know yourself fully. Identify what needs to change, and what needs to grow. Your reflection should be one of success, happiness, and fulfillment.

Day Five: The Mirror of Expression
Your social media, the profiles you've crafted—what do they say about you? Do they reflect your happiest moments and your best memories? Ensure the message you display is one of joy and of a life well-lived. Let your digital reflection be as authentic and optimistic as your real self.

Day Six: The Mirror of Aspiration
Reflect on your skills and your talents. What excites you? Build upon these. Let your hobbies and interests be a reflection of your innermost desires. Cultivate them, let them flourish, and watch as your reflection grows into the person you aspire to be.

Day Seven: The Mirror of Purpose
Finally, reflect on your purpose. All that you've observed, all that you've learned, culminates here. Your purpose is not just a reflection; it's the source of your light. Embrace it, live it, and let it shine through every aspect of your life. This is your challenge, your mission—seven days to transform the reflections around you into beacons that guide you to your true purpose. Start today, and let each reflection reveal a greater truth about who you are and who you are meant to be.

Remember, you are the architect of your reflections. Shape them with intention, courage, and an unyielding pursuit of excellence. Your life is a masterpiece waiting to be realized. Go forth and let your reflections illuminate the path to your destiny.

Chapter 6
Dream Again

"You can either sit around and look up at the stars or you can get up and become one.
Billy Alsbrooks

Now change is a slow and often grueling process. It's not like growth that we can witness and marvel at as we see our children blossom or our skills advance. Change is a silent, subtle force that unveils its full magnitude only when we look back at the distance we've covered from where we started. When I rewind the memories of my younger years, I can vividly remember the dreams and aspirations I had when I was 13 years old. I remember my favorite songs, movies, and TV shows when I was a teenager. I can remember what I wanted to be and look like at 21 years old because 21 was grown to me. I remember longing for a sleek, all-black Lamborghini and envisioning myself in a three-piece suit, working in a high-rise building overlooking the city skyline. I dreamt of being a man of success and substance. And I know you, too, must have dreamt of being someone extraordinary, someone who defies the odds and touches the sky.

As we grow up, we often find that these dreams, these glimpses of our future selves, don't greet us as we had hoped. We wander, we stumble, and we yearn for something that seems elusive and distant. But let me tell you, these dreams are not mere illusions. They are invitations, beckoning us to become the best versions of ourselves. Our future selves are not strangers; they are mirrors of our untapped potential, our purpose, our true calling.

Do you remember the vision you had of yourself as an adult? Do you remember the character traits, the qualities you wanted to embody? These were not mere fantasies; they were the seeds of your destiny, planted deep within your soul. It's time to nurture these seeds, cultivate our hidden strengths, and step into the shoes of our future selves. Embrace the journey, for it is through the arduous path of change and growth that we uncover our true selves. Dare to be audacious, to challenge the status quo, and to forge a path that leads you to the person you were always meant to be.

Let your dreams guide you. Let your purpose fuel you. And let the vision of your future self inspire you to become the extraordinary individual that lies within. The journey of change is a test of our resolve, our grit, and our tenacity. But if we remain steadfast in our pursuit, we shall emerge as the masters of our destiny, the architects of our lives, and the living embodiment of the dreams that once danced in the minds of our younger selves. So let us embark on this remarkable journey together and let the winds of change carry us to the heights of our greatness.

Today, I ask you to take a walk down memory lane, to delve into the depths of your past and unravel the dreams, aspirations, and fears of your younger self. For this first exercise, I want you to find an old picture of yourself from the age of 13 to 15 years old, a time when the world was full of possibilities, and your heart was brimming with hope.

Now, I want you to dive deep into the memories of those yesteryears. Feel the energy, the dreams, the hopes, and the fears of that young soul staring back at you from the photograph. This is not just an exercise; it's a journey into the heart of who you were, who you are, and who you can become. As you gaze upon that image, I want you to write out the answers to the side of the photo. This isn't about short, one or two-word answers. No, I want you to open up about yourself. Unleash the floodgates of your memories, and let your words flow like a river, painting a vivid picture of your past.

Think about your dreams and the person you want to become. Write out each answer in a complete sentence. For example, "When I was a child, I wanted to grow up and be a ___, with characteristics of ___."

Let your words breathe life into your past aspirations; let them echo the voice of your younger self. Once you've answered these questions, I want you to reread your entire entry. Read it like an autobiography, a story of a life lived and a life yet to be lived. As you read, you'll start to see patterns, connections, and threads that weave together the tapestry of your life. This exercise is not just about understanding your past; it's about illuminating your future. It's about realizing that the child in that photo, with all their dreams and fears, is still a part of you. And that child, that younger self, has the power to inspire and guide you towards your true potential. So, embark on this journey, dive deep into your past, and emerge with a clearer understanding of your true self.

1. What dreams did you have of being an adult?
2. What character traits did you see for your future?
3. What character traits did you have then?
4. Who was your role model then?
5. Who were your friends?
6. What type of character traits did your friends have?
7. Who were your enemies, people you didn't like?
8. What were your enemies' personality traits?
9. What did you love to do and love to play?
10. What did you hate to do and hate to play?

Let's take a moment to reflect, to look back at the photograph of our younger selves. That image captures more than a moment in time; it holds the essence of our dreams, the blueprint of the life we yearned to build. As we stand here today, let's honor that vision by asking ourselves the hard questions. When you gazed into the future, what did you see? Was it the halls of academia, the courtroom's thrill, or the boardroom's buzz? Whatever it was, it was your heart's true calling. It was the career that would make your pulse race and your spirit soar.

Dreams don't just materialize; they are the fruits of labor, the results of the education, training, and skills you've woven into the fabric of your being. Have you pursued those avenues of growth? Have you honed those skills that would set you on the path to your dreams?

And let's talk about love – the kind of partnership that elevates and inspires. The spouse you envisioned, what qualities did they possess? Were they driven, compassionate, a beacon of professionalism? Understand this: the partner you dreamt of is a reflection of the person you aspired to be. To attract that kind of love, you must first cultivate it within yourself. You must embody the qualities you admire – the seriousness, the education, the creativity. Ask yourself, would the partner of your dreams be drawn to someone lazy or childish? Or would they seek someone who mirrors their dedication and zest for life?

So here we are, with the wisdom of adulthood and the clarity of hindsight. It's time to align our actions with the aspirations of our youth. It's time to embrace the discipline that will propel us forward, to make the choices that reflect our highest selves, and to make the decisions that will lead us to the life we've always wanted. Remember, the relationship you desire, and the career you dream of, they're not out of reach. They are simply waiting for you to rise to the occasion. They are waiting for you to become the person who can claim them with confidence and pride.

So let's make a promise, here and now, to that hopeful teenager in the photograph. Let's commit to living a life that would make them proud. A life filled with purpose, passion, and the love of a partner who is every bit the equal we hoped to find. Be the architect of your destiny. Be the love you wish to receive. Be the change you want to see in the world. This isn't about casting judgment or dwelling on past mistakes. It's about acknowledging the chasm between who you are and who you aspire to be, and taking bold, decisive steps to bridge that gap. It is only when we confront our shortcomings and when we acknowledge our unfulfilled potential, that we can begin to chart a course toward greatness. So, my friends, as you reflect on the dreams of your younger self, let them serve as a beacon, a guiding light that illuminates the path ahead. Embrace the journey of self-discovery, growth, and transformation, and let the fire within you burn bright, fueling your quest to become the person you were always destined to be. Remember, your story is still being written, and every day presents a new opportunity to shape the narrative, redefine your path, and embrace the extraordinary potential that lies within. The journey will not be easy, but it will be worth it, for the person you were meant to be is just waiting to be unleashed.

Take a moment and look back. Look at that old photo of yourself. What do you see? You see a child with dreams, aspirations, and a vision for the future. You saw yourself as an adult, didn't you? Did you see yourself wanting to be more courageous, less aggressive, desiring more friendships, aspiring to be smarter, and more outgoing? You knew what you liked and what you needed to gain to become who you truly wanted to be. Now, let's take a moment to assess. How much of that vision did you accomplish? This isn't about comparison or meeting some societal standard. It's about authenticity. It's about being true to who you are.

There might be traits that seem impossible for you to embody now. Maybe it's impossible for you to bully someone else, or to stand in front of a crowd and give a speech or stand by while an injustice is happening and do nothing about it. But remember, the word 'impossible' is often just a mental barrier we've erected. Embrace that impossibility. Accept it. It's in the face of the impossible that we find our true potential, that we push our boundaries, that we become more than we ever thought we could be.

Reflect on your childhood traits. Which ones did you never lose? Which ones did you improve on? These are the essence of who you are. These are the strengths you've built over a lifetime. Remember, you are not defined by what you lack, but by what you have and what you can do. You are not defined by your failures but by your triumphs. And every day is a new opportunity to achieve, to grow, to become the person you've always wanted to be.

For the third question, look at your picture and at that child you once were. What were the character traits you had then? Were you an extrovert basking in the glow of social interaction, or an introvert, finding solace in solitude? Was that child-friendly or standoffish? Was that child good, bad, quiet, talkative? I want you to be brutally honest with yourself because this is not about who you are now, but about who you were then. Remember the compliments that were showered upon you. What were they? Were they about your kindness, your intelligence, your creativity? Remember the things that people said you were good at. Was it solving puzzles, playing a sport, or perhaps painting a picture? Remember the personality traits that people admired in you. Was it your resilience, your patience, your courage? But also remember the hurtful teases, the mocking laughter, the pointing fingers. What were they about? Was it about your shyness, your clumsiness, your simplicity? Remember how you felt, remember the tears, remember the pain. But also remember how it made you stronger, how it shaped you, and how it defined you.

Remember the duality of your personality. Remember how you were one person with your friends, perhaps cursing and clowning around friends, and another person with your teachers and adults, possibly being polite and respectful. Remember the rebellion, the rudeness, the disrespect to people you felt deserved it. But also remember respect, politeness, and obedience to those who earned it from you.

Now, imagine that child standing in front of you. What would you say to that child? Would you scold them for their mistakes, or would you praise him or her for their strengths? Would you befriend that child, or would you turn away in disgust? Would you be proud to call that child a reflection of yourself, or would you deny any association?

If that child made no changes, if there was no life-changing event in your youth, who would that child be today? Would that person be a friend of yours or an enemy? Would you like that person, or would you despise him or her? These are the questions that you need to ask yourself. These are the questions that will help you understand who you were, who you are, and who you will be. These are the questions that will guide you on your journey of self-discovery and self-improvement. So, take this journey. Dive deep into your past, confront your demons, and celebrate your victories. Because it is only by understanding our past that we can truly understand our present and shape our future.

For the fourth question, knowing who your role model was, lets you know who you looked up to. I want you to take a moment and think about your role models. Who were they? Celebrities, athletes, parents, siblings, teachers, or someone from your community? There was something about them that spoke to you, that resonated with you. It might have been their wealth, their respect, their power, their coolness, or the responsibilities they held. You may not have known what it was then, but as an adult, you should see it now. You admired the way they carried themselves. You found yourself imitating them, whether it was their speech, their style, their walk, or their sayings. And some of those imitations have become a part of you, haven't they?

Someone may have taken you under their wing, taught you new things, and introduced you to new ideas and perspectives. This person may have become a role model to you. When you were in their presence, you got to see their friends and know their influences.

They gave you advice, told you stories of what they did when they were your age, and guided you on what you should or should not do.

So, I want you to write down all these things. Write down who your role models were, what their influences were, and what their perspective of the world was. Write down the advice they gave you, and the stories they told you. Write down everything you can remember. Because these are the things that have shaped you, that have made you who you are today. And these are the things that will guide you, that will inspire you, that will motivate you to become the best version of yourself.

Remember, it's not about having the money for the clothes, the car, or the house that your role model had. It's about embodying the qualities that you admire in them. It's about living the values that they stood for, it's about becoming the person that you looked up to. So, take this journey of self-discovery, embrace your past, learn from your role models, and use their wisdom to shape your future. Because you have the power to become your role model, to become the person that others look up to.

The fifth and sixth questions ask, Who were your friends? There is an old saying that says, "You are who your friends are," and "You are a collective sum of every friend that you have ever known."

Think back to your childhood and your school days. Who were your close-knit friends? The ones you sat with at lunch, walked home with, talked on the phone, shared secrets with, and invited to parties.

These were not just people you spoke to or joked with, but your true friends. Write out their names. Some may still be your friends to this day. It should be a short list, no more than six or seven, and definitely under ten.

Now, think about your qualities and personality traits. Find the ones that you commonly share with these friends, the ones that you can say are true aspects of yourself. Do you still have those qualities? Do your friends still have the same qualities? As we grow and evolve, there are always personality traits we lose along the way. Some of these losses may have been for survival, or perhaps a new and better trait took its place. What qualities did you lose? Why did you lose them? What qualities did your friends lose? Understanding why we are attracted to certain personalities can help us understand ourselves better. It can help us grow, evolve, and become the best version of ourselves.

Remember, we are not defined by the qualities we lose but by the qualities we choose to nurture and the friends we choose to keep. So, let's celebrate our friendships, our shared qualities, and our unique journey of self-discovery. In the end, we are all a beautiful tapestry of the friends we've made, the experiences we've shared, and the qualities we've nurtured.

As you ponder these questions, remember that understanding our past relationships is key to forging stronger, more meaningful bonds in the present. By recognizing the qualities we once cherished in others, we can nurture those aspects of our personalities and seek out friends who share and celebrate them. The friendships of our youth may fade, but their impact endures, shaping the people we have become and the values we hold dear. So, embrace the memories, cherish the lessons, and let the echoes of those childhood bonds guide you toward the connections that will enrich your life today. Remember, you are the architect of your destiny, and in understanding who you were, you can better navigate the path towards who you are meant to be.

Next was knowing your enemies and their traits, knowing what type of people you don't get along with, and their personality traits let you see more of yourself. Let's take a moment to reflect on the adversities we've faced, the challenges that have shaped us, and the people who have stood against us. Just as our closest friends have nurtured our growth and forged our character, our adversaries, too, have played a crucial role in defining who we are today.

Think back to your childhood, to those who opposed you, who sought to dim your light or deter you from your path. Recall the traits that set them apart, the qualities that made coexistence a struggle. Did their aggression or disrespect ignite a fire within you, spurring you to fight for justice and fairness? Or perhaps their indifference and apathy were a stark reminder of the empathy and compassion we must all strive to embody.

Now, consider those who stand in opposition to you today. Are their qualities reminiscent of those childhood rivals, or have the challenges evolved with time? Pause to examine the reasons for their animosity. Do they resent your success or envy your determination? Or is it your integrity and unwavering principles that incite their disdain? Reflecting on these questions, we must ask ourselves if we've allowed these adversaries to shape us for the better. Have we used their disdain as fuel to propel us forward, or have we been lured into becoming the very thing we once despised? For it is in the crucible of conflict that our true character is revealed, and the choices we make in the face of opposition will forever define our legacy.

In the tapestry of our lives, even those who stand against us have a part to play. They force us to confront our fears, to question our assumptions, and to defend the values we hold dear. In recognizing their role, we can choose to rise above their negativity, transforming their opposition into an opportunity for growth and self-discovery.

As we move forward, let us remember that understanding our adversaries is not about dwelling on past conflicts or rekindling old wounds. It is about recognizing the lessons they've taught us and the strength we've gained in overcoming their challenges. It is about forging a path towards a brighter future, one in which we can coexist with those who challenge us, striving for unity and understanding even in the face of adversity. Together, let us embrace the wisdom born of our struggles and use it to light the way toward a more compassionate, more resilient, and more united world. For it is in the trials we've faced and the obstacles we've overcome that we find the strength to create a better tomorrow for ourselves and for generations to come.

The ninth question asked, What did you love to do in your childhood? Looking at that picture of yourself, you may have been on your way to do that activity, coming from it, or in the midst of it. What type of joy did you get from it? Do you still practice that activity today? What about the genre of the things that you like? Look upon that childhood photograph, that frozen moment in time, and allow it to transport you back to a world of wonder and possibility. Recall the activities that ignited your spirit, the hobbies, and interests that brought you unbridled joy. Whether it was the thrill of competition in sports or the exhilaration of artistic expression, embrace the memories of that youthful enthusiasm and let it rekindle your passion for life.

As you journey through these recollections, ask yourself if those childhood loves still burn within you today. Have you nurtured those early talents, or have the demands and expectations of adulthood overshadowed them? It's never too late to reawaken the dreams of your youth and breathe new life into the passions that once fueled your soul. Consider, too, the genres and forms of entertainment that captivated your young mind. Did the tales of horror and suspense send shivers down your spine, or did the bright colors and whimsy of animated stories bring a smile to your face? Reflect on the hours spent immersed in these worlds and the lessons they imparted. Remember, the stories we tell and the heroes we admire reveal volumes about our values and aspirations.

It's also essential to contemplate the influence of the screen, the vast sea of information and imagery that has become a fixture in our lives. Were you swept up in the tides of primetime television, or did you forge your path, charting a course through books, music, and the arts? As we grapple with the omnipresence of media in our modern world, we must ask ourselves if we control the screens or if the screens control us. Now, turn your gaze to the world around you, to the individuals and communities that captured your heart and imagination. Were you drawn to the energy and rhythm of hip-hop culture or the intellectual pursuits of scholars and scientists? Did you find solace in the embrace of friends who shared your interests, or were your passions seen as strange and misunderstood?

In reflecting on these questions, let us remember that our unique blend of talents, interests, and values sets us apart, defining our place in the rich tapestry of humanity. It is not enough to merely acknowledge these gifts; we must embrace them, nurture them, and use them to create the change we wish to see in the world.

Let us embark on this journey of self-discovery with courage and determination. Let us rediscover the joy and wonder of our youth, rekindling the flames of our passions and unleashing our true potential upon the world. Together, we can create a brighter future, one where our dreams become reality, and our unique gifts are celebrated for the treasures they truly are.

Focus on this with as much razor-sharp detail as possible, and if you are still doing it well and love it today. Remember, we are not defined by what others think of us, but by what we think of ourselves. So, let's choose to embrace our passions, our interests, and our talents. Let's choose to be true to ourselves and to pursue what brings us joy. Because, in the end, we are all a product of our choices, our experiences, and our passions.

Now for the last question, What did you hate to do? What were the things you dreaded to even think about doing? What were the tasks or experiences that filled you with unease or apprehension? By recognizing and understanding these aversions, we can glean invaluable insights into the fabric of our being. As you consider these trials, ask yourself how you navigated those turbulent waters. Did you confront your fears head-on or seek solace in the company of those who shared your trepidation? Our chosen strategies reveal much about our inner strength and resilience.

Recall, too, the moments when you rallied against the forces of injustice or stood firm against the oppressive tides of negativity. Were there times when you refused to partake in gossip or choose compassion over judgment? In these moments, we discover the guiding principles that define us and the values we hold most dear.

As we delve deeper into these experiences, let us acknowledge the environments and situations that made us feel uneasy. Did the confines of indoor spaces stifle your spirit, or were you daunted by the prospect of large gatherings and bustling crowds? In recognizing these challenges, we can better navigate our paths toward growth and understanding.

In the end, it is our shared struggles and the alliances we forge in the face of adversity that serve as the cornerstones of our character. By acknowledging our past challenges and the values that guided us through them, we can build bridges of empathy and compassion, ensuring that no one faces these trials alone.

As we move forward together, let us remember the lessons of our youth, embracing the challenges that await us with courage, resilience, and a steadfast commitment to uplifting one another along the way. In the words of Maya Angelou, "You may encounter many defeats, but you must not be defeated. It may be necessary to encounter the defeats, so you can know who you are, what you can rise from, and how you can still come out of it."

These choices, these dislikes, and these fears, all shape us into who we are today. They help us understand ourselves better. They help us grow, and they help us make better choices for our future. Remember, we are not defined by what we hate or fear, but by how we respond to them. So, let's choose to respond with courage, with understanding, and with the determination to be better. Because, in the end, we are all a product of our choices, our experiences, and our fears.

Reflecting on our childhood selves, we can see who we truly were, who we subconsciously wanted to be, and who we have become. This is an additional step in finding ourselves and our purpose. Take a moment to reflect on the intricate dynamics of your family, the ties that bound you to your parents, and the love that nurtured your spirit. Consider the roles your parents played in your upbringing and the unique bonds you forged with each of them. Whether you grew up in a single-parent household or navigated the complexities of shared custody, your experiences have shaped your understanding of love, trust, and resilience.

Embrace these lessons and allow them to serve as a foundation upon which you can build a future filled with empathy and compassion. As you journey deeper into the recesses of your past, acknowledge the siblings who shared your joys and sorrows and the unique roles each of you played within your family.

Consider your family dynamics. Were you an only child or the youngest sibling? Did you receive more, less, or extra attention than your siblings? Were you jealous or indifferent? What was the reason the sibling got extra attention? Did your siblings share the same parents, or were they more or less athletic, smarter, or more popular than you? Were you the workhorse of the house as an only child? What secrets did you keep? Why were they secrets at all? These are all pieces of the puzzle that make up who you are.

Remember, no one knows the thoughts you had about yourself and the world around you but yourself. Was the life you lived alright? Did you hate your childhood and want something better for yourself, for your mother, or your siblings? You may have grown up in a poor neighborhood and wanted to move into a suburban house when you grew up. These experiences shape us, they mold us into the individuals we become.

We are not defined by our past, but by how we respond to it. So, let's choose to respond with courage, with understanding, and with the determination to be better. Because in the end, we are all a product of our choices, our experiences, and our past.

Reflecting on your teenage self, What is the final conclusion that you have? Who were you then? What route did you know you should have taken, but did not? What are you proud that you took on? Did you become your image of your future self? This exercise is not meant to bring up bad memories or make you sad or mad. It's meant to be therapeutic, meditative, relaxing, and eye-opening. You must remember all memories, good and bad, achievements and regrets, to fully understand your makeup and your inner self. Subconsciously, you have a true understanding of your childhood self and your past self. In this moment of introspection, let us be kind to ourselves, for we are all works in progress, ever evolving and adapting to the ebbs and flows of life. By cultivating self-awareness and compassion, we lay the groundwork for personal growth and a more profound understanding of our place in the world.

Now, let's move on to your current self and know who you truly are today. Remember, we are not defined by our past, but by how we respond to it. So, let's choose to respond with courage, with understanding, and with the determination to be better. Because in the end, we are all a product of our choices, our experiences, and our past.

Chapter 7
Stepping Into The Greatness That You Are

"Your consistency must outlast the world's ignorance of who you truly are."
Billy Alsbrooks

'm going back to that image of my 21-year-old self that I had at the age of 13. That 21-year-old me wasn't the image that I had for myself as a teenager, but at the age of 21, I found that the greatness that was coming to me wasn't denied, just only delayed because I had an image of a 30-year-old me at the age of 21. I had a new vision of my future self being a man of integrity, stylish, suave, sharp, financially free, and happy. Again, my future self sent me an invitation to come to a greater self, into a higher self, and that at the age of 21, there wasn't a failure, but a stepping stone and a launching pad.

Now that I am well past the age of 30, and I look back at my old self, I can say that I am 1,000,000 miles from that old me. I'm 1,000,000 miles away from that alcoholic dead-beat, that marijuana head, that bum loser, that club hopper and that money blower. I am 1,000,000 miles away from being a screw-up, but I still have 1,000,000 miles more to go because change is never-ending.

Now, there is a certain picture of you when you're in your twenties. You're in some clothes or haircut that's out of style now. Maybe you're a different size and character, and when you look at that picture of your old self, do you remember that day exactly? Do you remember your thoughts on that day? Do you remember wanting to be something greater or doing something better than what you were doing then? Does that person you envision proudly live here today? If not, it is time to look at yourself in the mirror and look yourself in the eyes the way you look someone else in the eyes when you command respect; then ask yourself why and what it is going to take to become that person.

These are the photos that you would use for your next exercise in finding yourself. Place them to the side and look at them deeply with razor-sharp focus. Note the clothes you wore, the way you wore them, the background surroundings, and your facial expressions. Deeply dig into your memories and answer these questions. At the crossroads of your past and present, you stare into the eyes of a younger you, a version brimming with potential, dreams, and aspirations. Look closer, beyond the outdated hairstyle and clothes that no longer fit. Beneath the surface, that individual yearns for something greater, something transformative.

Now, pause and reflect on the journey between that moment frozen in time and the person you have become. Do you recall the path you've traveled, the lessons learned, and the dreams you've chased? Have you reached the pinnacle you once envisioned, or have you settled for less than what you truly desire? It's time to reignite the fire within. Dare to lock eyes with your reflection, commanding respect as you confront the innermost corners of your soul. Dive deep into those memories, embrace the experiences that have shaped you, and ask yourself the hard questions. What will it take to transform into the person you've always dreamed of becoming?

As you embark on this powerful journey of self-discovery, let that old photograph serve as a guiding light—a beacon illuminating the aspirations of your younger self. Study every detail, every nuance, and every emotion etched upon your face. Allow the memories to flood your consciousness as you redefine your path forward. Now is the moment to merge the past with the present, to weave a tale of resilience, determination, and unrelenting growth. Embrace the challenge of personal evolution and watch as the world unfolds before you, brimming with infinite possibilities. You are your destiny's architect; it's time to design the life you've always desired.

Now, at this age, you have a better understanding of the world. Reflect on your younger self, the one who was just beginning to grasp the complexities of the world and society. You had your notions of what was cool and what was corny. You knew what you stood against and what intrigued you the most. At this age, you have a better understanding of the world and society. You had your ideas of what was cool, what was corny, what you rebelled against, and what interested you the most. So, looking at that young adult, you will learn much more about yourself. Let's go over and see what we can find for young adults.

This exercise is not just about reminiscing. It's about understanding how far you've come and how much you've grown. It's about recognizing the journey you've undertaken to become who you are today. As you gaze upon the image of your young adult self, you are presented with a priceless opportunity to delve deeper into the complexities of your own identity. Explore the nuances of your past and unravel the mysteries that lie within your evolving psyche. Seek to comprehend the motivations that drove your passions and your eagerness to challenge the world around you.

Let us embark on an introspective journey through this pivotal period of growth and transformation. Examine the choices you made, the influences that shaped you, and the dreams that fueled your ambition. So, let's delve into the past, not to dwell there, but to learn from it. Let's explore the experiences, the triumphs, the failures, and the lessons of that young adult. Because in understanding our past, we gain insights into our present and can better shape our future. Remember, every step you've taken has led you to where you are now. And every step you take from here will lead you to where you want to be. Embrace the journey, for it is in the journey that we truly find ourselves.

For the first question, now that your world has changed and school is over, what dreams and goals did you have then? Do you still want to be the same thing at the age of 21 that you dreamed of as a teenager? Did you grow out of your childhood dream? For instance, I knew a guy who, when we were kids, wanted to be a garbage man so badly, but once he was in high school, he gave that dream up. Likewise, I knew a girl who wanted to be an astronaut so badly, mainly because we live in Houston, the Space City, and going to NASA on field trips. But later, she found out that it wasn't just being an astronaut but that she really wanted to be the first black female astronaut. Actually, Mae C. Jemison became the first black female astronaut. This girl that I knew gave that dream up. Now, she's trying to become the first black female governor of Texas.

As children, we dream of becoming police officers, secretaries, firefighters, stay-at-home parents, or nurses. But as we grow and our world expands, we often find that these careers no longer suit us. Our interests shift, our passions evolve, and we discover new paths that align more closely with our dreams. So, take a moment to reflect on your journey. Look back at your past, not with regret, but with understanding and gratitude. Each step you've taken, each dream you've pursued, has shaped you into the person you are today. And remember, no matter how far you've come, there's always room for growth because the journey to becoming the best version of ourselves is never-ending. Embrace the journey, for it is in the journey that we truly find ourselves.

For the next question, When you were at the age of 5 to 15 you were trying to understand the world around you, right? You were also into something that sparked your interest. Maybe it was working on cars with your dad, brother, or uncle. Think back to the time when you were just starting to get your feel for the world around you and knowing culture and social politics. Maybe it was bikes, hunting, fishing, training pets, fixing broken equipment, video games, or doing hair. Whatever it was, it was something you had real-world experience and knowledge in, something that went beyond book knowledge. You might have been the life of the party, the shoulder to cry on, the comedian, the hustler. You might have set trends that people followed and put together parties that everyone had to attend. You might have been the person who always matched the right people with each other, hooked people up, and was a great networker.

Now, take a moment to reflect on that one thing that fits you. Write it down. Ask yourself, how much more have you been using it, improving it, and utilizing it? Can you put it to use elsewhere as a career today? Remember, the skills and experiences you've gained over the years are not just hobbies or pastimes. They're a part of who you are. They're a testament to your growth, resilience, and adaptability. And they can be the foundation for your future success.

So, don't discount your past. Embrace it. Use it as a stepping stone toward your future because every experience, skill, and piece of knowledge you've gained along the way is a tool in your toolbox. With the right mindset, determination, and strategy, you can use those tools to build the career, life, and future you've always dreamed of.

Now, for the third question, What was the thing you did that people complimented you on? What were the things that they said you were good at doing? This is not what you think you're good at or what you think you are better at than other people, although they may be the same. But this is only what other people said you were the best at. Was it your fashion sense or your taste in art, or did you get compliments for being so brave, helpful, and calm under pressure? Think about the skills and talents people gave you the most compliments on. You may have heard someone tell you that you are good at something. You need to do a blog, YouTube, podcast, or a particular subject. Perhaps someone has constantly asked you for your aid in a particular area that you do naturally. Do people go to you for your expertise on consistent subjects? This is something that can be your purpose.

Let's talk about the currency of compliments. It's not just about feeling good. It's about recognizing the value you bring to the table. When people compliment you, they're not just being nice but identifying your unique selling proposition. Whether it's your fashion sense, artistic flair, or ability to stay calm under pressure, these are not just passing comments. They are the market's way of validating your expertise. And when you hear the same thing from multiple sources, that's a signal. It's time to monetize that talent. If you've been told you're good at something, whether it's your strategic thinking, creative content, or leadership skills, don't just brush it off. Take it to the bank. Share your knowledge, vision, and voice with the world because what comes naturally to you can be your biggest asset. But let's not ignore the flip side. If you've been advised to have more confidence or to be more open, don't dismiss it. Embrace it. These are the areas that, once improved, can skyrocket your success.

Have you ever been called over to meet someone new, maybe a friend of a friend, a cousin of a friend, a new relative, or someone else? From your encounter, you got a certain vibe, and you made assumptions about them because you didn't know them before. What did you learn about the character, personality, traits, and talents that they presented to you? They showed themselves to you. Likewise, you were unknown to them, and you made an impression on them. This was the moment of truth, where what you've learned about their character, personality, traits, and talents was presented to you. They revealed themselves, layer by layer, just as you did. It's a mutual unveiling of souls, where impressions are formed, and the foundations of relationships are built. But here's the twist: what others know of you is the persona you've projected, whether you did so with intention or without even realizing it. It's the image you've painted of yourself, with each stroke representing your actions and words. Yet, there's more to the canvas of your being. Some talents and potentials remain hidden, waiting for someone to uncover them.

Think about it. You've seen a talent in someone else that they hadn't recognized in themselves. It was an unexplored territory, a hidden gem that, once revealed, they embraced wholeheartedly. And just as you've been the catalyst for others, they've been the same for you. They've spotted a spark in you, a raw, untapped potential that you hadn't yet discovered. Reflect on the feedback you've received over the years—the comments about your traits, talents, skills, and personality. These aren't just passing remarks; they're insights into the essence of who you are. They're the echoes of your impact, the signature of your presence. In the grand narrative of life, we often overlook our potential. We become so accustomed to the image we present that we forget the power that lies within us. But remember, the most impactful version of you is not the one that's been carefully curated for the world to see. It's the one that's brimming with untapped potential. It's the one that's waiting to be set free.

So, take a moment to consider the possibilities. What if you could harness that potential? What if you could ignite that spark within you and let it grow into a blazing fire of passion and purpose? The impact you could have is limitless. Imagine discovering a talent in someone that they never recognized in themselves. It's like uncovering a hidden gem that, once polished, gleams with potential. You've been there, too. Others have seen a spark in you, a glimmer of untapped potential that you were oblivious to. They've mirrored a version of yourself ripe with possibility, a version that you might not have dared to acknowledge.

Recall the words that have been echoed to you repeatedly, the common thread in the tapestry of feedback you've received. These are not just idle compliments; they are clues to the parts of yourself that resonate most with the world. They are the signposts pointing toward the impact you are meant to make. In this journey of self-discovery, we must be willing to explore the uncharted territories within us. We must be open to the perspectives of others, for they can often see the mountains of potential that we mistake for molehills. In this exchange of insights, we find the courage to step into our power, embrace the full spectrum of our abilities, and make an indelible mark on the world.

As you navigate the waters of self-revelation, remember that the most impactful version of you is waiting just beneath the surface. It's time to dive deep, to bring forth the talents that have been whispering your name, and to let the world see the brilliance that has been there all along.

I remember when a friend of mine invited me to join Toastmasters. He said, "You have good topics of conversation and viewpoints. Why don't you try Toastmasters?" Initially, I declined, believing I was right to stay in my comfort zone. However, he persisted, echoing the common statements about my viewpoints, ultimately leading me to accept the invitation to Toastmasters. I stayed on, avoiding the old habit of dropping out and quitting.

Now, I may not be the best speaker or motivational speaker, but a talent within me was discovered that I didn't know myself. I never would have tried or pursued it on my own until someone else, who didn't know me at first but learned about me, pointed it out. Similarly, you may have observed some bad characters, ugly attitudes, or negative personalities in people and thought, "If this person just changed this, let go of that, or improved on this, they could be less untenable." Now, what were those traits that people recognized in you?

Remember, every interaction is an opportunity to showcase who you are. What you present to the world, both consciously and subconsciously, shapes your personal brand. And sometimes, it takes someone else's fresh eyes to reveal a talent or a passion you didn't realize you had. So, ask yourself: What have people consistently said you excel at? What have they seen in you that you haven't leveraged yet? These are not just random observations; they are your edge in a competitive world. It's time to embrace those strengths, to lean into them, and to let them guide you to your true calling. It's time to transform those compliments into a business strategy, a career trajectory, or a life mission. Let's not wait for the world to recognize our worth. Let's show it what we're made of. Let's turn our unseen potential into our greatest victory.

We are mirrors reflecting the collective wisdom of those who have seen in us what we often fail to see in ourselves. We've all been there, at the crossroads of external expectations and internal aspirations, where the voices of many echo the same sentiment about our untapped potential. "You need more confidence," they say as if to awaken the dormant lion within us. "Be more open," they urge, hinting at the vast skies we could soar if only we spread our wings. It's not the isolated advice of a passing acquaintance that we must heed, but the chorus of those who consistently see the same spark in us.

Remember the times when you were introduced to someone new? That moment of uncertainty, where first impressions are the only currency of judgment. They didn't know you, and you didn't know them, yet in that exchange, a revelation of character occurs. It's in these encounters that we present ourselves, consciously or subconsciously, painting a picture of who we are to the world. And what about the talents we see in others that they are blind to? Just as we have illuminated paths for them, others have shone a light on our hidden strengths. The common thread in their observations is a testament to what lies within us, waiting to be harnessed. So, let us take a moment to reflect on the recurring themes in our lives, the consistent feedback that forms a pattern, revealing our true capabilities.

For the fourth question, What were the things you did for money? Did those jobs or side hustles push you more toward your dreams and goals? Were the jobs somewhat related to the things you enjoy? Did you take on a job strictly for the money? Working jobs strictly for financial gain is acceptable if you use the money to fund your dreams or pursue your goals. However, dedicating eight hours a day, over 40 hours a week, to something that does not advance the skills you want or need to achieve your goals or dreams can be a significant waste of time. It's a detour in the wrong direction. Were you immersed in something that gave you great pleasure? That was your dream? Or was it a job you never considered, but being in it made you change your focus to a new goal?

For the fifth question, Who were the people that you dated, and what types of relationships did you have? Were they committed, long-term relationships, or short flings lasting from one week to one month? Who usually initiated the breakups, you or your partner? What key traits did you possess that attracted partners? What were the common compliments your dates gave you—was it about your looks, your hustle, your muscles, your brains, your money, your reputation, your status, your family, your personality, or your power? Did you pursue the business that you wanted? What attracted you to your dates? Did you receive anything just because they liked you? What qualities did you appreciate in your partners? Was it their intelligence, their attitude, their humor, their wealth? Did you share the same interests, or were you shallow and only went for looks? Being with the wrong person can affect your outlook on life. What types of people rejected you? Were they the pretty, stuck-up, gold diggers, or similar? You might be okay with that, but what if those who were smart, self-respecting, talented go-getters rejected you, and only the lazy, jobless, unmotivated ones liked you? Do you see how your partners can help define who you are?

Write down every name and why you were together, what you shared, what you created, and what you need to improve on, not only in relationships but also for yourself.

In the grand adventure of life, the relationships we forge are more than mere interactions; they are the crucibles within which our greatest strengths are forged, and our deepest vulnerabilities are revealed. Tony Robbins, a maestro of motivation, understands that each person we invite into our lives holds a mirror up to our soul, reflecting not just who we are but who we have the potential to become. So, who were the architects of your emotional landscape? Were they the steadfast builders of long-term commitments, laying brick by brick the foundation of a shared future? Or were they the artists of the ephemeral, sketching in bold strokes the contours of a passion that burned bright and fast? And when the time came to part ways, who was the sculptor of that decision? Whether it was you or them, each farewell carved a new path for growth.

Reflect upon the magnetism you possess, the traits that drew others into your orbit. Was it the aesthetic of your form, the relentless drive of your ambition, the intellectual depth of your thoughts, or the gravitational pull of your financial success? These attributes, reflected in the compliments of your dates, are but the surface of your vast potential. Did you chase the business of your dreams with the same fervor that you pursued the hearts of others? What was the spark that ignited your desire for those you chose to date? Was it the gift of their admiration or the alignment of their dreams with yours? The qualities you value in them—be it their intellect, their spirit, their wit, or their resources—mirror the values you hold dear.

Yet, let us not overlook the profound lessons etched in the fabric of rejection. The dismissal by the superficial or the ambitious is not a verdict on your worth but a compass pointing you toward greater self-awareness. What if the ones who saw your worth were the ones who challenged you to rise, while those who turned away were simply unable to see the giant within you? This is your moment of transformation.

Document the journey of each relationship, the shared dreams, the co-created wonders, and the areas ripe for improvement. For it is in the crucible of our connections that we discover the raw materials to build our ultimate destiny. Embrace the power of your relationships as the catalysts they are. Let them be the force that propels you to unleash the giant within, to step into your greatness, and to shape a destiny that is not just about success, but significance. With intense motivation, let this reflection be the spark that ignites the unstoppable force of your potential.

Now, for the next question: What did you do in your free time? When you were in your twenties, what activities did you engage in during your relaxing time? It's important to note that relaxing time is different from free time. Free time refers to the period you dedicate to practicing and studying toward your dreams or goals without monetary compensation. Did you spend it coding, DJing, making music, shopping, developing games, watching instructional YouTube videos, researching topics on the web, studying subjects related to your dreams, or attending conferences and conventions aligned with your goals? It's essential to understand what you do in your free time and whether it's something you've always done and always wanted—something you can't live without, or if it's subject to diminishing returns. Just because you enjoy something immensely doesn't necessarily mean it's your purpose; it could simply be a hobby. For instance, I recognize that I'm talented in the art of drawing, but it doesn't extend beyond being a hobby and a stress reliever for me. I never considered becoming a professional artist because I prefer to create what I want, rather than what someone else might expect from me, as a true professional artist would. Similarly, I realize that writing is not my purpose, but I used to write about my purpose to reach more people and touch more lives with what I'm passionate about.

Now that you are an adult and have put away childish things, what new interests have you gained? What grown-up things do you now enjoy at this age of independence, with no boundaries and your own choices? What are your interests? What topics and subjects interest you now that didn't when you were a child or teenager? Things and subjects that may have seemed boring or not even on your radar as a teenager, but now that you've matured and understand the world more, they captivate you more than anything else. You also need to recognize the things that you don't like anymore, the things you've put away as childish. At this age, those things could include, no longer getting mad and losing your temper, no longer seeing money as the sole means for everything, finding religion, no longer judging others by their appearances, old friends who no longer share the same insights as you, and, no longer basing someone's intelligence on whether it matches your own.

Write down the things that you don't want to do. If you know that you have a big heart, admit that you're not selfish or stingy. Conversely, if you are selfish and want everything for yourself, acknowledge that you are not big-hearted and that you are not a charity for others. If you are gullible and always say yes to all requests, admit and accept that you are gullible. If you do not like to take chances or gamble on investments and only go with the sure thing, low risk, and low rewards, then accept the fact that you are not a risk taker. If you are not good at managing money, admit that you need an accountant or CPA, and learn to manage your own finances. Now, list all your interests and likes, and find out which ones fit you best. If there is more than one, you can combine them into a collective interest.

What are you truly afraid of? This question delves deeper than mere phobias. It's about the fears that hinder progress and prevent us from moving forward. I'm not referring to the fear of death, heights, snakes, or spiders, but rather to those fears that cause anxiety, emotional stress, and worry, like fear of facing an authority figure, which may be daunting to some, or defending your views to superiors, which is intimidating to others. Some people are afraid to spend money. Some men hesitate to approach high-value women; similarly, some women feel intimidated by powerful, high-value men. These fears can hold a person back from their destiny. Many fear emotional pain, embarrassment, humiliation, and vulnerability. We all have something we're afraid of. I was afraid of being embarrassed and humiliated, and these fears kept me from my destiny so many times that I had no choice but to confront them head-on. Surprisingly, it wasn't as bad as I thought, although it was still challenging for my self-esteem.

Some have been so deeply hurt that they fear becoming attached to someone or having someone become too attached to them, to the point where they sabotage relationships that could have been fulfilling. Some even fear being themselves, changing their attitudes, suppressing their true thoughts, and biting their tongue to avoid hurting others because they fear the consequences of authenticity. Then some fear success, worrying that if they accumulate too much wealth or excel too far, they will lose friends who are not yet successful, or they will attract too many people interested only in their money. You can see how the fear of success can hinder you from fulfilling your destiny.

On the flip side of the fear of success is the fear of failure. When a person fears failing at what they do best, it can subconsciously discourage them, preventing them from living out their purpose, their destiny. It can keep them from submitting to contests, publishing, auditions, tryouts, opening a shop, or taking whatever first step is needed to fulfill their dream. Fearing that you will not make the cut, secure the deal, or even fear being second or not placing at all can greatly hinder you.

When I first embarked on my artistic journey, I was surrounded by a sea of art contests. Everywhere I looked, there were opportunities to showcase my work. Yet, I was plagued by self-doubt. I compared myself to the artist around me, the one who was teaching and showing me how to draw. I felt I wasn't as good. One day, I asked him, "Why don't you submit to the contest? You don't even have to submit your original if you could have a JPEG." His response was disheartening. It was, "I would never win anyway. Those contests are rigged."

Despite his pessimism, I decided to take a leap of faith. I submitted some of my work. To my surprise, I was placed in magazine contests and won prize money. Although I never won first place or the grand prize, it was a victory nonetheless. I had proven to my teachers, and more importantly to myself, that fear of failure had kept them and could have kept me from exposure, extra money for our work, and being part of the vibrant art world and culture. This experience taught me a valuable lesson about fear. We all have something we are afraid of, something we don't like or feel is beneath us. It could be a fear of rejection, a fear of failure, or even a fear of success. These fears can hold us back, keep us from taking risks, and prevent us from realizing our full potential.

So, I encourage you to confront your fears. Write out the things you are afraid of doing, fearful of feeling, and afraid of experiencing and why. This exercise can help you understand your fears better. It can help you realize that these fears are not insurmountable obstacles but challenges that you can overcome. Remember, fear is not a sign of weakness. It is a sign that you are human, that you are alive. Embrace your fears, for they are the stepping stones on your path to growth and self-discovery. As you confront and overcome each fear, you will find yourself growing stronger, more confident, and more in tune with your true self. So, take that first step. Confront your fear. Embrace it. And watch as you transform it into a stepping stone towards your destiny.

For the ninth question, when you look at that photo of your younger self, can you identify and recall your weaknesses and strengths? Consider how much your strengths have compensated for your weaknesses, and vice versa, how much your weaknesses have overshadowed your strengths. What you perceive as a weakness is not necessary for you to experience failure, but these are the very things that are essential to fulfill your purpose. Thus, a weakness for someone else might not be a weakness for you but rather a strength, and what may be your strength could be a weakness for another person.

You have the power to transform your weaknesses or to harness them as strengths. Being arrogant may be a weakness in a friendly meeting or social gathering, but it can be a strength in board meetings, courtrooms, and when closing deals in sales. A weakness such as being timid can become a strength of cautiousness in buying and selling stocks, real estate, and any investment. Similarly, the weakness of being shy can translate into the strength of being an excellent listener, which is invaluable for investigative detective work and intelligence gathering. You must find a way to convert your weaknesses into strengths. The tendency to be frugal, often seen as being a cheapskate, can be a strength when it comes to saving for compound interest and building a solid credit score. When you stare into the eyes of your younger self, captured in a frozen moment, what do you see? A reflection of innocence, perhaps, or a raw portrait of your nascent strengths and weaknesses. It's a confrontation with the past that begs a critical question: How have your inherent traits carved the path you walk today?

In the relentless pursuit of success, society has spoon-fed us the narrative that weaknesses are the kryptonite to our Superman, the Achilles' heel to our warrior spirit. But what if I told you that this is a grand illusion, a mirage in the desert of conformity? Let's dismantle this myth. Your so-called weaknesses, the traits you've been conditioned to curse, are not just stumbling blocks; they are the hidden keys to unlocking a realm of untapped potential and the timidness that once made you second-guess your every move. It's the cautious strategy that now guides your hand in the high-stakes game of decision-making. The arrogance that might have cost you friendships is the same unyielding confidence that commands boardrooms and seals deals.

In a world that preaches the gospel of strengths, I challenge you to rebel. To recognize that what makes you falter in one arena can make you invincible in another. It's a dance of duality where your weaknesses are not fixed points on a map but shifting sands that can be molded and redefined. Consider the shy child who preferred the company of books over people. In the silence of their solitude, they honed the art of listening, a skill that now serves them as the linchpin of investigative work, psychology, or the perfect life partner, where hearing what isn't said is just as crucial as what is.

This is the art of turning the tables on weakness, of flipping the script so that what once hindered you now propels you forward. It's about embracing the full spectrum of your character and recognizing that every flaw is a potential strength in disguise. So, look again at that photo of your younger self. See beyond the surface. Your journey isn't about shedding your weaknesses; it's about transforming them, wielding them as weapons, and marching into battle with a newfound sense of purpose. Ultimately, it's not the absence of weakness that defines us; it's how we harness it to fuel our ascent to greatness.

When I first began practicing martial arts, I was punch-shy, scared to get hit in the face. Others saw this fear as a weakness, but my instructor, my sensei, viewed it as a strength and a defensive tactic. To dodge, block, slip, and counter are all part of the defense. When you're afraid of getting hit, you're more inclined to evade and counterattack compared to those who brace themselves for the impact. They are seen as strong for being able to take a punch without flinching, ducking, or dodging. My fear of being hit became a defensive strength, making me hard to hit and almost impossible to catch. Because I trained my reflexes and my natural aversion to punches, I improved to the point where my strength became the envy of all my peers.

When I was younger, I wanted to be the best at whatever I did, no matter how new I was to the subject. Even when facing veterans and champions, I believed that I was just as capable. I knew I could master the topics I initially failed at if I kept at them. I excelled, but for those pursuits that didn't resonate with me and that seemed unworthy of my effort, I abandoned them. I lacked passion for those subjects, activities, or topics. You can fail and still feel good, knowing that you are improving and that it's all part of the practice. So, what were those things that you really didn't like? Were they the ones that caused more discouragement than a sense of achievement the more you engaged with them? I can imagine that coding and computer science captivate Mark Zuckerberg more than basketball, and for LeBron James, basketball offers a greater sense of fulfillment than computer science and coding. It's not about which skill set is more important or valuable than another person's; it's about finding your purpose in what you do and allowing others to find theirs in what they do.

Picture this: You're young, ambitious, and hungry for success. You step into the ring, a novice among titans, but in your heart, you're a giant. You're not just playing the game; you're rewriting the rules. This isn't about ego; it's about knowing that within you lies the same potential that propels the greats. Now, fast forward. You've tasted defeat, sure, but each setback has sharpened your edge. You've learned that mastery isn't a gift; it's a conquest. And as for those pursuits that didn't light a fire in your soul, you dropped them like hot coals. Why? Because life isn't about collecting trophies in areas that leave you cold. It's about igniting passion. So, ask yourself, what drags you down? What saps your spirit? If it doesn't serve you, cut it loose. Zuckerberg found his battlefield in algorithms and code, not on the hardwood. LeBron soars in stadiums, not in server rooms. And you? You're carving your legend.

Remember, it's not a competition of skill sets; it's a symphony of individual purposes. Find your rhythm, your arena, your crusade. And when you do, pursue it with a relentless force that is uniquely yours. Because at the end of the day, it's not about fitting into someone else's shoes—it's about forging your path and leaving footprints that others will aspire to follow. Now, go out there and make your mark. Be unapologetically you. That's not just success; that's a legacy.

Now, you need to check your ego at the door, swallow your pride—even if it gives you indigestion—and admit the things that you are not good at or what is not good for you, no matter how much you feel it defines you. You may want to be a great singer, but if everyone tells you that you can't hold a note correctly, you will have to accept the fact that you can't sing and will not be a singer. However, all is not lost because, although you can't be a singer, you can become a songwriter, a song producer, or even a DJ or VJ. You can be an A&R, CEO of a label, or create an app or website strictly for singers.

Likewise, you will have to acknowledge and accept the characteristic traits that don't belong to you, that you want to define you. You may think that you are respected, but you may be feared. You may feel that you are celebrated when you're just being tolerated. Pick two things to improve on and become greater at doing. Practice them over and over again until you get what you want, so you can have what you need: peace, happiness, and purpose. Don't give up on studying yourself. Don't give up on your plan. Keep it up, keep it up, keep it up until you achieve your goal. By now, you should have more than the things that bring you happiness, that you want to be around daily and enjoy doing, even if you weren't paid for it.

Step out of the life you are accustomed to, to live out the life you want to have. You develop muscles without some resistance, without some heavy weight on you. Now, your purpose isn't something to take lightly. It can't be taken lightly. These are heavy subjects that weigh down on you. You have to keep pushing through. Keep pushing forward in your purpose, developing your talent for destiny.

CLOSING

"Your calling isn't something that somebody can tell you about. It's what you feel. It is the thing that gives you juice. The thing that you are supposed to do. And nobody can tell you what that is. You know it inside yourself."
Oprah Winfrey

"If you can't figure out your purpose, figure out your passion. For your passion will lead you right into your purpose." —
Bishop T.D. Jakes

You're standing at the edge of a dark, winding path, a mystery wrapped in shadows. Your feet are planted firm, but there's a hesitation in the air. You know this journey won't be easy, but you've got a fire in your gut telling you it's worth the trouble. The road ahead is full of twists and turns, and the city's underbelly sprawls out around you like an old, familiar friend. Every corner's got a secret, every alleyway a new challenge to overcome. But you're no stranger to this game. You've walked these streets before, and you know how to navigate the darkness.

As you push forward, the world shifts and changes, mirroring your inner struggles. The rain pours down, blurring the lines between reality and memory, and you find yourself facing obstacles that test your mettle. You're climbing mountains, crossing rivers, and navigating treacherous cliffs, each one a reflection of the demons you're battling within. But through it all, you keep pushing, keep fighting, and as you emerge from the darkness, you can feel yourself growing stronger, more resilient. The path becomes clearer, and the sun breaks through the clouds, illuminating your destination like a beacon in the night. And there, at the peak of your journey, you stand tall, staring out at the world with newfound clarity. You've faced your demons, conquered your fears, and discovered a sense of purpose that drives you forward. The world may be a dark and dangerous place, but you've emerged from the shadows with a fire in your soul and the knowledge that you've got what it takes to make it in this town.

It was a hell of a journey and one that would leave its mark on anyone who dared to embark on it. But for those who did, the reward was worth it: a sense of purpose, a reason to keep pushing forward, even when the world seemed to be against them. And as the image faded away, leaving nothing but the memory of that lone figure, standing tall and proud against the backdrop of a world in flux, one thing was clear: the journey to find your purpose in life is never easy, but it's always worth it in the end.

We all have an undeniable force within us, an immense potential waiting to be unleashed. It's time to tap into that power and propel ourselves to new heights of personal growth and success! The framework for this transformative journey lies in the realization that you hold the key to your destiny. You are the architect of your life, and when you choose to take charge, incredible things can happen. Start by setting clear, ambitious goals that reflect your deepest passions and aspirations. Once you've defined your objectives, create a roadmap for achieving them. Break down your goals into manageable steps, and commit to taking action every day.

Embrace challenges as opportunities for growth. Remember, it's not about avoiding obstacles; it's about facing them head-on and using them as stepping stones on your path to greatness. When you shift your mindset, seemingly insurmountable barriers become exciting chances to test your resolve and build your resilience. Foster meaningful connections with like-minded individuals who uplift and inspire you. Surrounding yourself with a supportive community can bolster your determination and provide valuable insights along the way. Learn from your experiences and continuously refine your approach. Each setback offers a lesson, and each triumph is a testament to your progress. Cultivate a growth mindset that embraces learning and adaptation, allowing you to make the most of every opportunity.

Above all, believe in yourself and your limitless potential. When you fully embrace your power, you'll find the strength and determination to overcome any challenge and create the life you've always dreamed of. So, go ahead – step into your greatness and make it happen!

Finding yourself is an act of fierce self-love and acceptance. Embrace every part of you, your story, your strengths, your struggles. They all weave together to create the magnificent tapestry of your individuality. And from that place of deep self-awareness, your purpose will begin to illuminate itself to you. Your purpose is the unique contribution that only you can make to this world. It is the expression of your values, your passions; your life experiences all coalescing. Hold that purpose up like a torch to guide you. It will steer you toward the choices, relationships, and impact that are distinctly yours to make. Allow yourself to be a masterpiece in progress. And in doing so, you will discover the unstoppable power and profound peace that comes from living profoundly in your purpose.

So, in my final farewell, congratulations, my friend! You've done it – you've reached the pinnacle of your journey, standing tall and proud as you survey the winding path that brought you here. Through determination and an unwavering commitment to self-discovery, you've uncovered the truth of who you are and the purpose that drives you. Your journey has been a testament to your strength and resilience. You've faced your fears head-on, transformed obstacles into opportunities, and tapped into the limitless potential that lies within you. You're a unique individual with remarkable talents and skills that set you apart from the crowd.

As you move forward into the next chapter of your life, remember the lessons learned along the way. Each challenge you've conquered has fortified your spirit and deepened your understanding of your purpose. With this newfound clarity, you're poised to make an extraordinary impact on the world around you. Embrace the future with open arms, knowing that you possess the power to shape your destiny and create the life you've always dreamed of. Your purpose is your compass, guiding you toward fulfillment, joy, and success. With passion, perseverance, and an unwavering belief in yourself, there's no limit to what you can achieve.

So go forth, champion, and let your purpose light the way. The world awaits your unique gifts, and it's your time to shine. Remember, you are the master of your fate, and with each step, you have the power to create a brighter, more meaningful future for yourself and those around you.

About The Author

Rashard Renfro is on a mission to inspire and empower individuals to unlock their full potential and achieve their dreams. With a passion for personal development and a relentless drive for success, Rashard's journey from adversity to empowerment serves as a beacon of hope for all who hear his message. Rashard Renfro is a visionary Graphic Designer and Hologram Creator with a unique talent for crafting immersive holographic light shows. With a keen eye for design and a passion for pushing the boundaries of visual art, Rashard has carved out a niche in the world of digital design. Born and raised in Houston, Texas, Rashard was faced with seemingly insurmountable challenges from the moment he entered this world, having nearly lost his life at birth due to a rare bleeding disorder called Glanzmann's thrombasthenia. Despite this difficult start, Rashard persevered. His journey took him through even darker times, as he spent 17 long years in prison from 2006 to 2023.

During these trying times, he never gave up hope that he would one day be reunited with the love of his life. Upon his release, there seemed to be a turning point as he reunited with her, and their love grew. They clung to the dream of a shared future together, and they became engaged. Yet, life's tribulations took their toll, and their bond eventually broke. She broke his heart and his spirit, proving that love is the ultimate contact sport. She emotionally bankrupted him so badly, even his feelings filed for Chapter 11. Rashard was left in the wake of heartbreak, with the pain of separation compounded by the knowledge that his very presence had caused the one he loved so deeply to break apart. But Rashard did not let this adversity break him. Instead, he took these experiences and turned them into a catalyst for growth and self-improvement.

Through unwavering dedication and a resilient spirit, Rashard emerged from these trials as a testament to the power of perseverance. Rashard's message revolves around the power of mindset, resilience, and self-belief. Drawing from his own experiences, he delivers impactful talks that resonate with audiences of all ages. Whether speaking to students, professionals, or community groups, Rashard's authenticity and passion shine through, leaving a lasting impact on those who hear him speak. In addition to his speaking engagements, Rashard is also an advocate for personal growth. He believes that by embracing challenges and adopting a growth mindset, anyone can create the life they desire. As Rashard continues his journey as an aspiring motivational speaker, he remains committed to helping others realize their potential and live their best lives.

Made in the USA
Columbia, SC
07 February 2025

52866732R00067